P · O · C · K · E · T · S

WORLD ATLAS

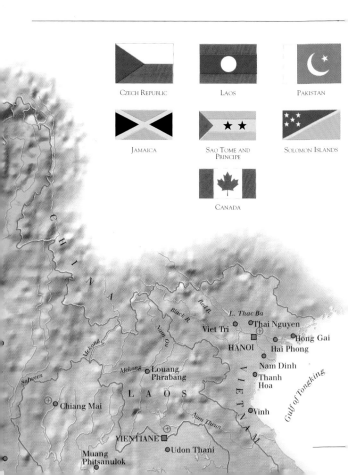

CZECH REPUBLIC

LAOS

PAKISTAN

JAMAICA

SAO TOME AND PRINCIPE

SOLOMON ISLANDS

CANADA

CHINA

Saween

Mekong

Nam Ou

Black R.

Red R.

L. Thac Ba

Viet Tri

Thai Nguyen

HANOI

Hong Gai

Hai Phong

Nam Dinh

Mekong

Louang Phrabang

LAOS

VIETNAM

Thanh Hoa

Chiang Mai

Nam Theun

Vinh

Gulf of Tongking

VIENTIANE

Udon Thani

Muang Phitsanulok

P · O · C · K · E · T · S

WORLD ATLAS

Written by
ESTHER LABI

DORLING KINDERSLEY
London • New York • Stuttgart

A DORLING KINDERSLEY BOOK

Editor	Esther Labi
Designer	Carlton Hibbert
Senior editor	Hazel Egerton
Senior art editor	Jacquie Gulliver
Editorial consultant	Joan Dear
Picture research	Lorna Ainger
Production	Ruth Cobb

First published in Great Britain in 1995
by Dorling Kindersley Limited
9 Henrietta Street, Covent Garden, London WC2E 8PS

Visit us on the World Wide Web at http://www.dk.com

Reprinted 1996, 1997

A CIP catalogue record for this book is available from
the British Library

ISBN 0 7513 5321 3

Colour reproduction by Colourscan, Singapore
Printed and bound in Italy by L.E.G.O.

CONTENTS

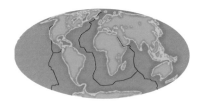

HOW TO USE THIS BOOK

THESE PAGES SHOW YOU how to use *Pockets: World Atlas*. The maps are organized by continent: North America, Central and South America, Europe, Africa, North and West Asia, South and East Asia, and Australasia. There is also an introductory section at the front and a comprehensive index at the back.

KEY TO ICONS
All the icons used in the Atlas are listed below.

THE ARTS

CLIMATE

COMMUNICATIONS

ENVIRONMENT

FLORA AND FAUNA

HISTORY

INDUSTRY

NATURAL FEATURES

PEOPLE

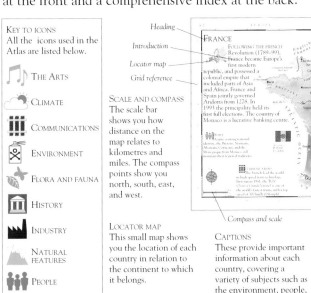

Heading

Introduction

Locator map

Grid reference

SCALE AND COMPASS
The scale bar shows you how distance on the map relates to kilometres and miles. The compass points show you north, south, east, and west.

LOCATOR MAP
This small map shows you the location of each country in relation to the continent to which it belongs.

Compass and scale

CAPTIONS
These provide important information about each country, covering a variety of subjects such as the environment, people, climate, and history.

INTRODUCTION

This provides you with an overview of the area or region and gives interesting facts about the country's climate, landscape, and political situation.

RUNNING HEADS

These remind you which section you are in. At the top of the left-hand page is the name of the continent. The right-hand page gives the country. This page on France is in the section on Europe.

This page on France is in the section on Europe.

Running head

Caption icon

Caption

Flag

FLAGS

The flag of each nation is positioned next to the country. Also included are population figures (**P**) and information about the official languages spoken in that area (**L**).

GRID REFERENCE

The letters and numbers around this grid help you to locate places listed in the index. See page 136 for an explanation on how to use this grid.

See page 136 for an explanation on how to use this grid.

GAZETTEER INDEX

A gazetteer index at the back of the book lists all the major towns, cities, rivers, mountain ranges, and lakes that appear in the book.

KEY TO MAPS

INTERNATIONAL BORDER	
DISPUTED BORDER	
STATE BORDER	
CAPITAL·CITY	SHING' D.C.
STATE OR ADMINISTRATIVE CAPITAL	LANT.
MAJOR TOWN	arlesto
AIRPORT	⊕
SEAPORT	⊛
RIVER	
CANAL	
WADI	
LAKE	
SEASONAL LAKE	

GUIDE TO MAP PAGES

EUROPE
54-55

NORTH AND
WEST ASIA
102-103

SOUTH AND
EAST ASIA
114-115

AFRICA
86-87

*INDIAN
OCEAN*

AUSTRALASIA
130-131

*ATLANTIC
OCEAN*

*SOUTHERN
OCEAN*

ARCTIC
OCEAN

Arctic Circle

ATLANTIC
OCEAN

NORTH AMERICA
20-21

PACIFIC
OCEAN

Tropic of Cancer

Equator

PACIFIC
OCEAN

CENTRAL AND
SOUTH AMERICA
40-41

Tropic of Capricorn

ATLANTIC
OCEAN

THE PLANET EARTH

EARTH, ONE OF nine planets that travel around the Sun, is part of the solar system within a galaxy called the Milky Way. The only planet within our solar system that supports life, Earth has sufficient light, heat, and water to support a wide range of plants and animals. The atmosphere protects the planet by filtering the Sun's rays.

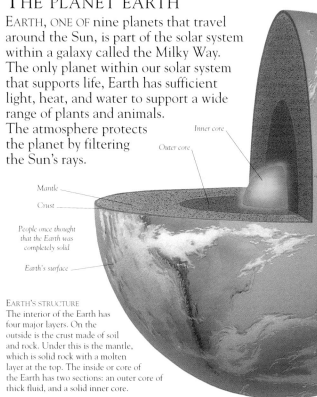

Inner core

Outer core

Mantle

Crust

People once thought that the Earth was completely solid

Earth's surface

EARTH'S STRUCTURE
The interior of the Earth has four major layers. On the outside is the crust made of soil and rock. Under this is the mantle, which is solid rock with a molten layer at the top. The inside or core of the Earth has two sections: an outer core of thick fluid, and a solid inner core.

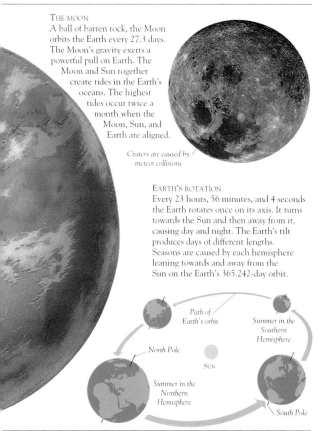

THE MOON

A ball of barren rock, the Moon orbits the Earth every 27.3 days. The Moon's gravity exerts a powerful pull on Earth. The Moon and Sun together create tides in the Earth's oceans. The highest tides occur twice a month when the Moon, Sun, and Earth are aligned.

Craters are caused by meteor collisions

EARTH'S ROTATION

Every 23 hours, 56 minutes, and 4 seconds the Earth rotates once on its axis. It turns towards the Sun and then away from it, causing day and night. The Earth's tilt produces days of different lengths. Seasons are caused by each hemisphere leaning towards and away from the Sun on the Earth's 365.242-day orbit.

Path of Earth's orbit

Summer in the Southern Hemisphere

North Pole

SUN

Summer in the Northern Hemisphere

South Pole

THE MOVING CRUST

THE EARTH'S CRUST is broken up into 15 plates in which the continents are embedded. Some countries lie in the middle of a plate, while others have a plate boundary through them. Forces in the Earth's mantle move the plates slowly around the globe, a process called continental drift. Rift valleys, ocean trenches, and mountains have all formed in areas where plates meet.

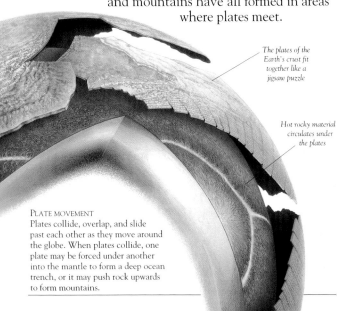

The plates of the Earth's crust fit together like a jigsaw puzzle

Hot rocky material circulates under the plates

PLATE MOVEMENT
Plates collide, overlap, and slide past each other as they move around the globe. When plates collide, one plate may be forced under another into the mantle to form a deep ocean trench, or it may push rock upwards to form mountains.

220 MILLION YEARS AGO
Scientists believe that about 220 million years ago the world's continents were part of one giant continent called Pangaea. Over the following 20 million years, it split into Laurasia and Gondwanaland.

100 MILLION YEARS AGO
Africa and South America separated 100 million years ago, breaking away from Antarctica. The Atlantic Ocean was created by a spreading ridge between North America, Europe, and Africa.

PRESENT DAY
Scientists can only guess what the world was like before Pangaea, but if the movement of plates continues, the Great Rift Valley will become an island and Africa and Europe will fuse.

SLIDING PLATES
The San Andreas fault, where two plates are sliding past each other, extends for 965 km (600 miles) in California, U.S.A. Movement between the plates is not steady and pressure builds up, causing earthquakes. About 90 per cent of earthquakes occur in the "Ring of Fire", around the Pacific plate.

CLIMATE AND VEGETATION

THE MAIN INFLUENCES on an area's climate are its distance from a large body of water, its height above sea level, and the amount of sunlight it receives. Rainfall and sunlight levels are highest at the equator, where the habitats with the most plant and animal life are found: rainforests, mangrove swamps, and coral reefs.

POLAR
Polar regions are so cold that few plants can survive. The treeless tundra regions of Siberia, Canada, Scandinavia, and Alaska support moss and lichens, as well as small flowers and shrubs during summer.

COOL
Coastal areas have less extreme climates than inland regions. Coniferous forests grow in cold northern Asia and North America. Warmer areas have forests of deciduous trees, which lose their leaves in winter.

WARM
Hot, dry summers and wet winters are typical of the Mediterranean region as well as parts of Southern Africa, the Americas, and Australia. Vegetation varies from treeless grasslands to open forests of trees and shrubs.

The world's largest remaining rainforest is in the Amazon Basin, Brazil

DESERT AND DRY LANDS
Arid and semi-arid lands cover more than 30 per cent of the Earth's land surface. Semi-arid regions scattered with grasses and scrubs are called savannah. Cold deserts, like the ice deserts of the Arctic and Antarctic, have no more rain than the Sahara.

TROPICAL
High temperatures and high rainfall are typical of the Tropics. The main difference between tropical and monsoon climates is the distribution of rainfall. Tropical rainforests near the equator depend on year-round rainfall.

The coniferous forests of Asia and northernmost Europe are called taiga

MOUNTAIN
Vegetation on the lower slopes depends on the climate zone in which the mountain is located. Mountains become colder with altitude and only hardy alpine plants grow above the treeline. Snow and bare rock occur above the snowline.

TROPICAL MONSOON
Tropical regions with distinct wet and dry seasons have a monsoon climate. Each year, the monsoon winds reverse their direction completely, forming the two seasons.

Gum trees, or Eucalyptus, have adapted to dry conditions

WORLD TIME ZONES

IMAGINARY LINES are drawn around the globe, either parallel to the equator (latitude) or from pole to pole (longitude, or meridians). The Earth is divided into 24 time zones, one for each hour of the day. Greenwich is on 0° meridian and time advances by one hour for every 15° of longitude east of Greenwich.

TIME ZONES
The numbers on the map indicate the number of hours which must be subtracted or added to reach GMT. When it is noon at Greenwich, for example, it is 11 p.m. in Sydney, Australia. Time zones are adjusted to regional administrative boundaries.

KEY TO MAP

⬤ MINUS HOURS

⬤ PLUS HOURS

◯ GREENWICH MEAN TIME

◐ DATE LINE

  TIME ZONES

GMT
Greenwich Mean Time (GMT) is the time in Greenwich, England. Clocks are set depending on whether they are east or west of Greenwich.

INTERNATIONAL DATE LINE
The International Date Line is an imaginary line that runs along the 180° meridian but deviates around countries.

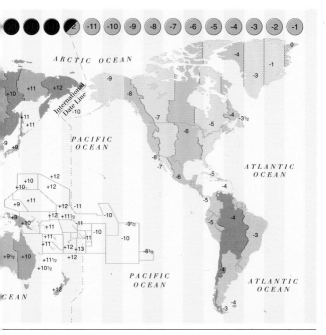

NORTH AMERICA

ARCTIC OCEAN

BEAUFORT SEA

Alaska
(to U.S.A.)

CANADA

GULF OF ALASKA

PACIFIC OCEAN

UNITED STATES

Hawaii
(to U.S.A.)

MEXICO

Greenland
(to Denmark)

BAFFIN BAY

HUDSON
BAY

LABRADOR SEA

ATLANTIC OCEAN

OF AMERICA

GULF OF
MEXICO

NORTH AMERICA
Canada and the United States of America
make up most of the continent. To the
south of the United States lie Mexico and
Central America. The northernmost part
of the continent sits in the Arctic Circle.
Greenland, to the northeast of Canada, is
the largest island in the world.

ALASKA AND
WESTERN CANADA

AT THE END OF the last ice age, people travelled from Asia into North America over the Bering landbridge, which connected the continents at present-day Alaska.

ARCTIC OCEAN

Bering Strait

BROOKS RANGE

Prudhoe Bay

BEAUFORT

St. Lawrence I.

Nunivak I.

St. Matthew I.

BERING SEA

ALEUTIAN ISLANDS

A L A S K A (U.S.A.)

Yukon

Porcupine

Fairbanks

Yukon

ALASKA RANGE

Dawson

Anchorage

Bristol Bay

Unmak I.

Unalaska I.

Unimak I.

Kodiak I.

Gulf of Alaska

WHITEHORSE

ROCKY MOUNTAINS

MACKENZIE MTS

JUNEAU

P A C I F I C   O C E A N

Queen Charlotte Is.

BRITISH COLUMBIA

Vancouver

Fraser

Vancouver

VICTORIA

🇺🇸

ALASKA
P 550,043
L English

INDUSTRY
Fishing, oil, minerals, timber. Railways were the key to the development of farming in western Canada. The U.S.A.'s biggest oil field is at Prudhoe Bay, Alaska.

CLIMATE
A polar climate prevails in the north; the south is warmer. The Pacific coast, near Vancouver, has the warmest winters, and temperatures rarely fall below freezing.

HISTORY
The U.S.A. bought Alaska from Russia in 1867 for $7.2 million. Many Americans thought this was a waste of money until gold was discovered there in 1896 and oil in 1968.

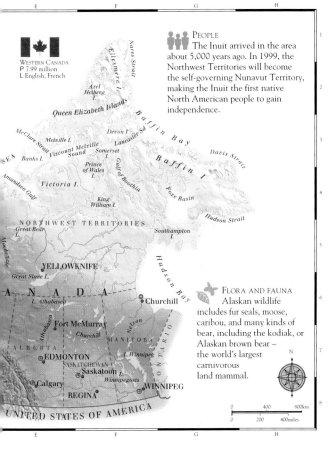

WESTERN CANADA
P 7.99 million
L English, French

Nares Strait

Ellesmere I.

Axel
Heiberg
I.

Queen Elizabeth Islands

Baffin Bay

McClure Strait Melville I. Devon I. Lancaster Sd

Viscount Melville Somerset Baffin I.
Sound I.

Banks I. Prince
of Wales
I.

SEA Davis Strait

Amundsen Gulf Victoria I. Gulf of Boothia

King
William I. Foxe Basin

NORTHWEST TERRITORIES Hudson Strait
Great Bear
L. Southampton
I.

YELLOWKNIFE

Mackenzie Great Slave L.

Hudson Bay

A N A D A

L. Athabasca Churchill

Fort McMurray
Athabasca Churchill Nelson

ALBERTA MANITOBA

EDMONTON L. Winnipeg
SASKATCHEWAN
Saskatoon Winnipegosis

Calgary REGINA WINNIPEG

UNITED STATES OF AMERICA

People

The Inuit arrived in the area about 5,000 years ago. In 1999, the Northwest Territories will become the self-governing Nunavut Territory, making the Inuit the first native North American people to gain independence.

Flora and Fauna

Alaskan wildlife includes fur seals, moose, caribou, and many kinds of bear, including the kodiak, or Alaskan brown bear – the world's largest carnivorous land mammal.

N

0   400   800km
0   200   400miles

EASTERN CANADA

ALTHOUGH IT IS the second largest
country in the world, Canada has a
relatively small population. Most
people live within 160 km (100
miles) of the U.S. border. Snowbound
for most of the year, the
Hudson Bay area is a
wilderness of
forests, rivers,
and lakes.

PEOPLE
The Vikings
were the first
Europeans to visit
eastern Canada in
about 986 B.C. They
settled for only a short
time before the Native
Americans drove them away.

INDUSTRY
Wood industries, oil, zinc,
nickel, hydro-electricity, uranium.
The area off the east coast called the
Grand Banks is one of the world's
richest fishing areas. Newsprint,
made from wood pulp, is a major
export from the Atlantic provinces.

Salisbury I.
Nottingham I.
Mansel I.

Inukjuak

Hudson Bay

Belcher Is.

MANITOBA

Severn

Winisk

C. Henrietta
Maria

James' Bay

Attawapiskat

Attawapiskat

ONTARIO

Albany

CANADA

Lake of the
Woods

L. Nipigon

Thunder Bay

UNITED   Lake Superior

STATES OF

Timmins

Sault
Sainte Marie

Sudbury

Ottawa

Lake Michigan

Lake Huron

AMERICA

TORONTO
Hamilton   Lake
                  Ontario

London

Windsor

Niagara
Falls

Lake Erie

UNITED

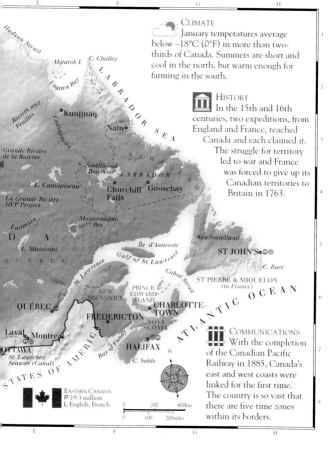

CLIMATE
January temperatures average below –18°C (0°F) in more than two-thirds of Canada. Summers are short and cool in the north, but warm enough for farming in the south.

HISTORY
In the 15th and 16th centuries, two expeditions, from England and France, reached Canada and each claimed it. The struggle for territory led to war and France was forced to give up its Canadian territories to Britain in 1763.

COMMUNICATIONS
With the completion of the Canadian Pacific Railway in 1885, Canada's east and west coasts were linked for the first time. The country is so vast that there are five time zones within its borders.

Hudson Strait

Akpatok I.   C. Chidley

Ungava Bay

Rivière aux
Feuilles   Kuujjuaq

L A B R A D O R   S E A

Nain

Grande Rivière
de la Baleine

Caniapiscau

Smallwood
Reservoir   L A B R A D O R

L. Caniapiscau   Churchill   Goosebay
La Grande Rivière   Falls
HEP Project

Eastmain   Manicouagan
Res.

D   A   Newfoundland

L. Mistassini   Île d'Anticosti   ST JOHN'S ●⊕⊕

Q U É B E C   Gulf of St.Lawrence   C. Race

St. Lawrence   Cabot Strait   ST PIERRE & MIQUELON
(to France)

NEW   PRINCE
BRUNSWICK   EDWARD
ISLAND   CHARLOTTE-   A T L A N T I C   O C E A N
TOWN

QUÉBEC ●⊕

FREDERICTON   NOVA
Laval ●   SCOTIA
Montréal ●   HALIFAX
OTTAWA ●⊕
St. Lawrence   Bay of Fundy
Seaway (Canal)   C. Sable

S T A T E S   O F   A M E R I C A

N

EASTERN CANADA
P 19.3 million
L English, French

0   200   400km

0   100   200miles

NORTHEASTERN STATES

WITH ITS RICH MINERAL resources and safe harbours, northeast America was the first area on the continent to be colonized by Europeans. In 1620, English pilgrims sailed on the *Mayflower* to settle in a region that is still called New England. During the mid-19th century, European immigrants settled in New York City and in other East Coast cities. Today, this region is the most densely populated and heavily industrialized area of the U.S.A.

CLIMATE
This area of the U.S.A. has a temperate climate, with warm and humid summers. However, the northeastern region, in particular, can experience very heavy snowfall from November to April.

NORTHEASTERN STATES
P 51.5 million
L English

PEOPLE
Northeastern Native American tribes, such as the Wampanoag, the Algonquin, and the tribes of the Iroquois League, were the first to come into contact with European settlers and explorers.

INDUSTRY
Oil, iron, steel, chemicals, maple sugar, blueberries, cranberries, fishing, tourism. Vermont is the main producer of maple syrup in the U.S.A. The stock exchange on Wall Street, New York City, is the largest in the world.

Niagara Falls

Lake Erie Buffalo

Erie

OHIO

PENNSYLVANIA

Pittsburgh

WEST VIRGINIA

APPALACHIAN MTS.

NATURAL FEATURES
Lying on the border between the U.S.A. and Canada, Niagara Falls were formed about 10,000 years ago. About 180,000 tonnes (tons) of water go over the falls every minute.

HISTORY
In 1621, the *Mayflower* pilgrims celebrated their first successful harvest. Thanksgiving is now an annual holiday, observed on the last Thursday in November.

FLORA AND FAUNA
The Appalachian Mountains are home to the opossum, North America's only species of marsupial, or pouched mammal.

CANADA

MAINE

Moosehead

Kennebec

Penobscot

AUGUSTA

L. Champlain

WHITE MTS.

MONTPELIER

ADIRONDACK MTS.

VERMONT

NEW HAMPSHIRE

L. Ontario

Rochester

Syracuse

Mohawk

Finger Lakes

ALBANY

NEW YORK

Connecticut

CONCORD

CATSKILL MTS.

Hudson

MASSACHUSETTS BOSTON

Springfield Worcester Cape Cod

CONNECTICUT PROVIDENCE

RHODE ISLAND

Waterbury HARTFORD

New Haven

Martha's Vineyard

Nantucket I.

Delaware

Paterson Bridgeport

Allentown Newark New York City

HARRISBURG TRENTON

Long I.

Susquehanna

Wilmington Philadelphia

MARYLAND

Newark

NEW JERSEY

DOVER

DELAWARE

ATLANTIC OCEAN

N

0   100   200km
0   50   100miles

SOUTHERN STATES

BY THE 19TH CENTURY, the wealth of the South was based on crops like tobacco, indigo, rice, and especially cotton, which was grown on large plantations by African slaves. The area is known today for New Orleans' jazz, Florida's Disney World, and the Kentucky Derby. The city of Washington, in the District of Columbia, was made the U.S. capital in 1800.

Mississippi Delta

CLIMATE
Summers are long and hot; winters are mild, but temperatures are generally warmer on the coast than inland. Southern Florida is tropical.

INDUSTRY
Soya beans, coal, peanuts, cotton, citrus fruits, tobacco, oil, tourism. Georgia grows half of the U.S.A's peanuts – most are used to make peanut butter.

THE ARTS
The French brought Mardi Gras to America in the early 1700s. Celebrated in many of the southern states, the most famous festival is held in New Orleans. Here parades last for a week before Mardi Gras Day, the day before Lent starts.

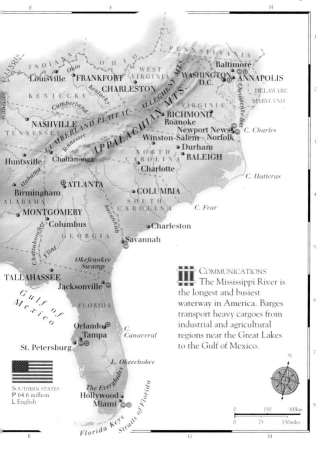

COMMUNICATIONS
The Mississippi River is the longest and busiest waterway in America. Barges transport heavy cargoes from industrial and agricultural regions near the Great Lakes to the Gulf of Mexico.

SOUTHERN STATES
P 64.6 million
L English

THE GREAT LAKES

THE STATES OF Indiana, Illinois, Michigan, Ohio, Wisconsin, and Minnesota, which all border on one or more of the five Great Lakes, are often called the industrial and agricultural heartland of the United States. The region is rich in natural resources, with large areas of fertile farmland on flat plains called prairies.

CLIMATE
The region around the Great Lakes has warm summers but quite severe winters, and parts of the lakes can freeze over. Minnesota, in particular, suffers from heavy snowstorms.

ENVIRONMENT
The Great Lakes – Ontario, Huron, Superior, Michigan, and Erie – together form the largest area of fresh water in the world. Heavy industry has caused severe water pollution, and in some areas it is dangerous to eat the fish or swim.

GREAT LAKES STATES
P 46.4 million
L English

INDUSTRY
Vehicles, coal, iron, grain, maize, cherries. Nearly half of the world's maize crop and a third of the cherry crop are grown in the Great Lakes region. Detroit is known as "motor city" because it is the centre of the U.S. car industry.

E F G H

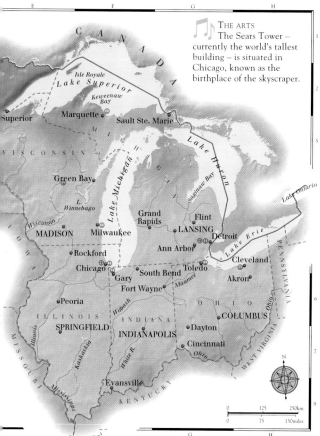

THE ARTS
The Sears Tower – currently the world's tallest building – is situated in Chicago, known as the birthplace of the skyscraper.

CANADA

Lake Superior

Isle Royale

Keweenaw Bay

Superior

Marquette

Sault Ste. Marie

MICHIGAN

Lake Huron

WISCONSIN

Green Bay

Saginaw Bay

Lake Michigan

Lake Ontario

L. Winnebago

Wisconsin

Grand Rapids

Flint

MADISON

Milwaukee

LANSING

Detroit

Lake Erie

IOWA

Rockford

Ann Arbor

Cleveland

PENNSYLVANIA

Chicago

South Bend

Toledo

Gary

Akron

MISSOURI

Fort Wayne

Maumee

Peoria

Wabash

OHIO

ILLINOIS

INDIANA

COLUMBUS

Ohio

SPRINGFIELD

INDIANAPOLIS

Dayton

Illinois

Kaskaskia

White R.

Cincinnati

WEST VIRGINIA

Ohio

N

Mississippi

Evansville

KENTUCKY

0   125   250km
0   75   150miles

CENTRAL AND MOUNTAIN STATES

THE GREAT Plains, the Rocky Mountains, and the Mississippi lowlands dominate the landscape of the Midwest. Once home to Native Americans and herds of bison, the Great Plains were settled in the 19th century by Europeans, who forced the Native Americans onto reservations and slaughtered the bison to near extinction.

HISTORY
Pioneers travelling to the West had to cross the Great Plains, which were known as the "Great American Desert". The last area to be settled, it is now a wealthy agricultural region.

CLIMATE
West of the Rockies, the summers are cooler and the winters are warmer. States on the Great Plains have an extreme climate, which can change quite suddenly and violently – blizzards, hail, thunderstorms, and tornadoes may occur.

CENTRAL AND
MOUNTAIN STATES
P 18.7 million
L English

NATURAL FEATURES
The Rocky Mountains extend through Canada and the U.S.A. for more than 4,800 km (3,000 miles). They divide North America and separate the rivers flowing west to the Pacific from those flowing east to the Atlantic.

FLORA AND FAUNA

Grizzly bears were once found west of the Black Hills in South Dakota. So many have been hunted that there are probably fewer than 800 grizzly bears left. Most are found in the mountains of Idaho and Wyoming.

INDUSTRY

Cattle, wheat, maize, oil, coal, natural gas, gold. Crop farming on the Great Plains of the Midwest is large-scale and mechanized. Closer to the Rockies, rainfall decreases and arable farming gives way to cattle ranching.

SOUTHWESTERN STATES

THE FIRST Europeans in the Southwest were the Spanish, who travelled north from Mexico. This resulted in a mingling of Spanish and Native American cultures in the region. Gold and silver mining and cattle-ranching attracted other settlers in the late 19th century, when this area became part of the U.S.A. after the Mexican War.

Map labels:
OREGON · IDAHO
BLACK ROCK DESERT
GREAT
Pyramid L.
Humboldt
Great Salt L.
Reno
CARSON CITY
L. Tahoe
BASIN
GREAT SALT LAKE DESERT
SALT LAKE CITY
NEVADA
Sevier L.
Bryce Canyon
Las Vegas
L. Mead
Grand Canyon
COLORADO PLATEAU
ARIZONA
Colorado
PHOENIX
SONORAN DESERT
Mesa
Tucson

NATURAL FEATURES

The Colorado plateau has some unusual landforms, including natural bridges and arches of solid rock. Over the past million years, the Colorado River has cut away the plateau, forming the world's largest river gorge – the Grand Canyon.

SOUTHWESTERN STATES
P 28.4 million
L English

HISTORY

At the end of the Mexican War (1846–48), the U.S.A. acquired Utah, Nevada, California, and parts of Arizona, New Mexico, Colorado, and Wyoming. One of the causes of the war was a border dispute between Texas and Mexico.

PEOPLE

Some of the earliest Native Americans lived in the Nevada area. Bones and ashes discovered near Las Vegas indicate that people may have lived there more than 20,000 years ago. Today, the region has the largest concentration of Native Americans in the country.

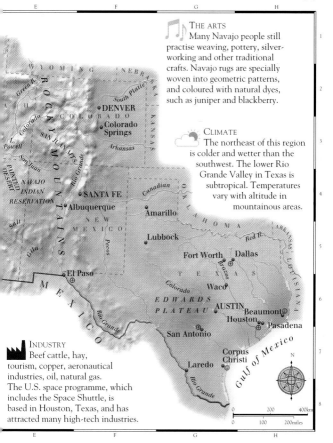

THE ARTS
Many Navajo people still practise weaving, pottery, silver-working and other traditional crafts. Navajo rugs are specially woven into geometric patterns, and coloured with natural dyes, such as juniper and blackberry.

CLIMATE
The northeast of this region is colder and wetter than the southwest. The lower Rio Grande Valley in Texas is subtropical. Temperatures vary with altitude in mountainous areas.

INDUSTRY
Beef cattle, hay, tourism, copper, aeronautical industries, oil, natural gas. The U.S. space programme, which includes the Space Shuttle, is based in Houston, Texas, and has attracted many high-tech industries.

WYOMING
NEBRASKA
Green R.
ROCKY
COLORADO
DENVER
Colorado Springs
South Platte
KANSAS
L. Powell
SAN JUAN MTS.
San Juan
Colorado
Arkansas
PAINTED DESERT
NAVAJO INDIAN RESERVATION
Rio Grande
SANTA FE
Albuquerque
NEW MEXICO
Salt
Gila
MOUNTAINS
Pecos
Canadian
Amarillo
OKLAHOMA
Lubbock
Red R.
ARKANSAS
Fort Worth Dallas
Brazos
El Paso
TEXAS
LOUISIANA
MEXICO
Colorado
Waco
EDWARDS PLATEAU
AUSTIN
Beaumont
Houston
Pasadena
Rio Grande
San Antonio
Corpus Christi
Laredo
Gulf of Mexico
Rio Grande

N

0   200   400km
0   100   200miles

PACIFIC STATES

ALL THREE STATES on the West Coast are major agricultural producers – Washington and Oregon supply one-third of the softwood timber in the U.S. and California produces half of the country's fruit and vegetables. Situated where two of the Earth's plates meet, the area suffers from earthquakes and volcanic activity. Mount St. Helens, dormant since 1857, erupted in 1980, losing some 400 m (1,300 ft) off its height.

NATURAL FEATURES
The lowest point in the western hemisphere is in Death Valley, 86 m (282 ft) below sea level. One of the driest, hottest places on Earth, the highest temperature, 57°C (135°F), was recorded there in 1913, and its average rainfall is only 38 mm (1.5 in) per year.

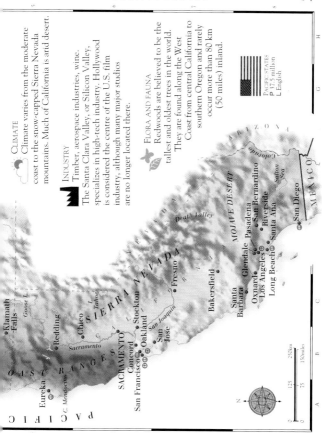

CLIMATE
Climate varies from the moderate coast to the snow-capped Sierra Nevada mountains. Much of California is arid desert.

INDUSTRY
Timber, aerospace industries, wine. The Santa Clara Valley, or Silicon Valley, specializes in high-tech industry. Hollywood is considered the centre of the U.S. film industry, although many major studios are no longer located there.

FLORA AND FAUNA
Redwoods are believed to be the tallest and oldest trees in the world. They are found along the West Coast from central California to southern Oregon and rarely occur more than 80 km (50 miles) inland.

PACIFIC STATES
P 375 million
L English

MEXICO

THE ANCIENT empires of the Maya and Aztec flourished for centuries before the Spanish invaded Mexico in 1519, lured there by legends of hoards of gold and silver. Mexico gained its independence in 1836, after 300 years of Spanish rule. Today, most Mexicans are *mestizo*, a mix of Spanish and Native American. Although Spanish is the official language, Native American languages such as Maya, Nahuatl, and Zapotec are also widely spoken.

CLIMATE

The Mexican plateau and mountains are warm for most of the year. The Pacific coast has a tropical climate.

Mexico
P 84.4 million
L Spanish

FLORA AND FAUNA

The Mexican beaded lizard and the gila monster are the only two poisonous lizards known. The largest of all cacti is the giant saguaro, which grows in the Sonora Desert to a height of more than 18 m (60 ft).

NATURAL FEATURES

The plateau of Mexico is enclosed to the west and east by the Sierra Madre mountain ranges, which occupy 75 per cent of the total land area. Mexico is so mountainous and arid in parts that only 12 per cent of the land is arable.

Map labels: UNITED STATES, Tijuana, Mexicali, Nogales, Ángel de la Guarda I., Hermosillo, Cedros I., Tiburón I., SIERRA MADRE, BAJA CALIFORNIA, Gulf of California, Culiacán, La Paz

E   F   G   H

ENVIRONMENT
Poor air quality is a problem in
Mexico City because it is surrounded by
mountains, which stop fumes from cars
and factories from escaping.

HISTORY
The remains of Mayan and
Aztec cities are found all over Mexico
and Central America. Mexico City is
built on the ruins of the Aztec
capital, Tenochtitlán.

INDUSTRY
Oil, natural gas, tourism,
minerals, brewing, agriculture.
Tourism employs nine per cent of
the workforce. Mexico is one of the
largest oil producers and supplies
one-sixth of the world's silver.

GULF OF AMERICA

Ciudad
Juárez

Bravo del Norte

Chihuahua

SIERRA MADRE ORIENTAL

Conchos

Rio Grande

OCCIDENTAL

M E X I C O

Monterrey

San Luis Potosí

Rio Grande de Santiago

Marías
Iss

Aguascalientes   Ciudad
Madero

León

Guadalajara   Poza Rica

L. Chapala

MEXICO CITY   *L. Texcoco*

Balsas   Puebla

SIERRA MADRE OCC SUR

Acapulco

P A C I F I C   O C E A N

Gulf of Mexico

Mérida

Campeche   Cozumel
                I.

YUCATÁN
PENINSULA

Bay of Campeche

Villahermosa

Coatzacoalcos

Oaxaca   Tuxtla
            Gutiérrez

BELIZE

GUATEMALA

*Gulf of
Tehuantepec*

Tapachula

N

0   200   400km

0   100   200miles

E   F   G   H

CENTRAL AND SOUTH AMERICA

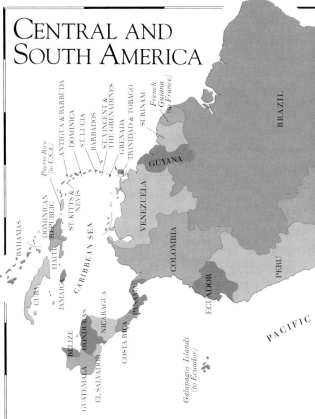

ANTIGUA & BARBUDA

DOMINICA

ST. LUCIA

BARBADOS

ST. VINCENT & THE GRENADINES

GRENADA

TRINIDAD & TOBAGO

Puerto Rico (to U.S.A.)

French Guiana (to France)

SURINAM

GUYANA

BAHAMAS

DOMINICAN REPUBLIC

HAITI

ST. KITTS & NEVIS

VENEZUELA

COLOMBIA

BRAZIL

PERU

CARIBBEAN SEA

CUBA

JAMAICA

BELIZE

HONDURAS

NICARAGUA

COSTA RICA

PANAMA

GUATEMALA

EL SALVADOR

ECUADOR

Galapagos Islands (to Ecuador)

PACIFIC

ATLANTIC OCEAN

BOLIVIA

PARAGUAY

URUGUAY

ARGENTINA

CHILE

Falkland Islands
(to U.K.)

OCEAN

CENTRAL AND SOUTH AMERICA

Until three million years ago, South America was an island with its own unique flora and fauna. The narrow Isthmus of Panama is the continent's only link to North America. South America's southernmost tip, Cape Horn, is only 970 km (600 miles) from Antarctica.

CENTRAL AMERICA AND THE CARIBBEAN

CENTRAL AMERICA FORMS a narrow land bridge linking North and South America. To the east lie the Caribbean islands, many of which are uninhabited.

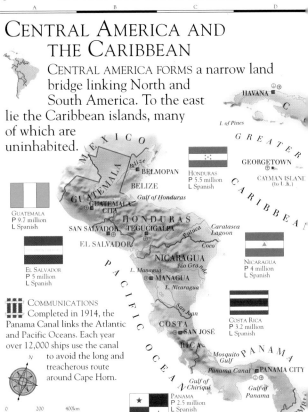

HAVANA

I. of Pines

GREATER

GEORGETOWN

CAYMAN ISLANDS
(to U.K.)

CARIBBEAN

HONDURAS
P 5.5 million
L Spanish

BELMOPAN

BELIZE

BELIZE

Gulf of Honduras

GUATEMALA
P 9.7 million
L Spanish

GUATEMALA
CITY

HONDURAS

SAN SALVADOR TEGUCIGALPA

Patuca   Caratasca
Lagoon

EL SALVADOR

Coco

EL SALVADOR
P 5 million
L Spanish

NICARAGUA

Rio Grande

L. Managua

MANAGUA

L. Nicaragua

NICARAGUA
P 4 million
L Spanish

COMMUNICATIONS
Completed in 1914, the Panama Canal links the Atlantic and Pacific Oceans. Each year over 12,000 ships use the canal to avoid the long and treacherous route around Cape Horn.

San Juan

COSTA

SAN JOSÉ

RICA

COSTA RICA
P 3.2 million
L Spanish

PACIFIC OCEAN

Mosquito
Gulf

PANAMA

Panama Canal PANAMA CITY

Gulf of
Chiriquí

Gulf of
Panama

N

0   200   400km
0   100   200miles

PANAMA
P 2.5 million
L Spanish

COLOMBIA

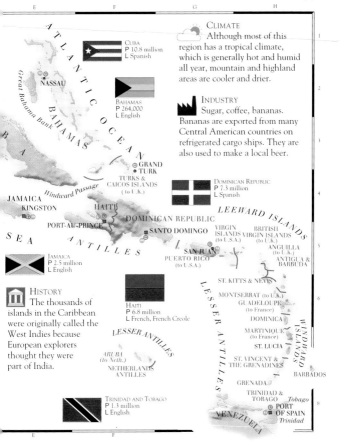

ATLANTIC OCEAN

CUBA
P 10.8 million
L Spanish

NASSAU

Great Bahama Bank

BAHAMAS
P 264,000
L English

CLIMATE
Although most of this region has a tropical climate, which is generally hot and humid all year, mountain and highland areas are cooler and drier.

INDUSTRY
Sugar, coffee, bananas. Bananas are exported from many Central American countries on refrigerated cargo ships. They are also used to make a local beer.

GRAND
TURK
TURKS &
CAICOS ISLANDS
(to U.K.)

JAMAICA
KINGSTON

Windward Passage

HAITI

PORT-AU-PRINCE

DOMINICAN REPUBLIC

SANTO DOMINGO

SEA

ANTILLES

DOMINICAN REPUBLIC
P 7.3 million
L Spanish

LEEWARD ISLANDS

VIRGIN
ISLANDS
(to U.S.A.)

BRITISH
VIRGIN ISLANDS
(to U.K.)

SAN JUAN
PUERTO RICO
(to U.S.A.)

ANGUILLA
(to U.K.)

ANTIGUA &
BARBUDA

JAMAICA
P 2.5 million
L English

ST. KITTS & NEVIS

MONTSERRAT (to U.K.)

GUADELOUPE
(to France)

HISTORY
The thousands of islands in the Caribbean were originally called the West Indies because European explorers thought they were part of India.

HAITI
P 6.8 million
L French, French Creole

DOMINICA

MARTINIQUE
(to France)

ST. LUCIA

ST. VINCENT &
THE GRENADINES

BARBADOS

LESSER ANTILLES

GRENADA

ARUBA
(to Neth.)

NETHERLANDS
ANTILLES

TRINIDAD &
TOBAGO

Tobago

PORT
OF SPAIN

Trinidad

TRINIDAD AND TOBAGO
P 1.3 million
L English

VENEZUELA

LESSER ANTILLES

WINDWARD ISLANDS

Northern South America

THE INCAS RULED MUCH of this area in the 15th century, and today large numbers of their descendants live in Peru, Ecuador, and Bolivia. In 1533, the last Incan emperor was executed by the Spanish, who colonized this region. The French, Dutch, and British later settled in the countries east of Venezuela, although all but French Guiana are now independent.

VENEZUELA
P 20.4 million
L Spanish

GUYANA
P 800,000
L English

SURINAM
P 425,000
L Dutch

CARIBBEAN SEA

Gulf of Venezuela

Santa Marta
Barranquilla
Cartagena
Gulf of Darién
PANAMA

Maracaibo
Barquisimeto
L. Maracaibo
Mérida
Medellín
BOGOTÁ
Buenaventura
Cali

Valencia
CARACAS
Barinas
Villavicencio

Margarita I.
Cumaná
Maturín
Ciudad Bolívar Ciudad Guayana

VENEZUELA

COLOMBIA
AMAZON BASIN

Magdalena
Cauca
Meta
Guaviare
Arauca
Apure
Orinoco

GEORGETOWN
New Amsterdam

PARAMARIBO

CAYENNE
FRENCH GUIANA
(to France)

GUYANA
SURINAM

Essequibo
Berbice
Courantyne
Marowijne

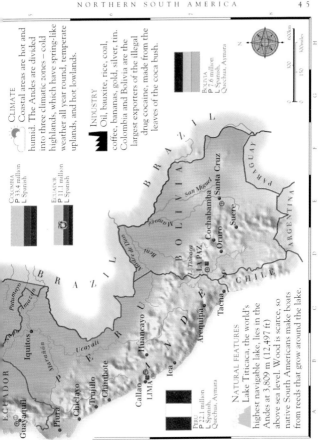

CLIMATE

Coastal areas are hot and humid. The Andes are divided into three climatic zones – cold highlands, which have spring-like weather all year round, temperate uplands, and hot lowlands.

INDUSTRY

Oil, bauxite, rice, coal, coffee, bananas, gold, silver, tin. Colombia and Bolivia are the largest exporters of the illegal drug cocaine, made from the leaves of the coca bush.

BOLIVIA
P 7.6 million
L Spanish,
Quechua, Aymara

COLOMBIA
P 33.4 million
L Spanish

ECUADOR
P 11.1 million
L Spanish

NATURAL FEATURES

Lake Titicaca, the world's highest navigable lake, lies in the Andes at 3,809 m (12,497 ft) above sea level. Wood is scarce, so native South Americans make boats from the reeds that grow around the lake.

PERU
P 22.1 million
L Spanish,
Quechua, Aymara

BRAZIL

OCCUPYING NEARLY HALF of South America, Brazil has the largest river basin in the world. Many Brazilians are descendants of Portuguese, who colonized Brazil in the 16th century, and Africans, who were brought to work on sugar plantations. Brazil's Native American tribes have little contact with the outside world. In 1992, the United Nations held its first Earth Summit in Rio, partly to highlight the destruction of the Amazon rainforest, the largest rainforest in the world.

PEOPLE

There were once about two million indigenous people living in Amazonia. Today only 50,000 remain. The survival of many tribes and their way of life is threatened by the destruction of the Amazon rainforest.

ATLANTIC OCEAN

Natal

Fortaleza

Teresina

Parnaíba

São Luís

Belém

SERRA PELADA

Santarém

Xingu

Tapajós

FRENCH GUIANA (to France)

SURINAM

GUYANA

VENEZUELA

COLOMBIA

Negro

Balbina Res.

Manaus

Madeira

Amazon

Purus

Solimões

Amazon

Juruá

AMAZON BASIN

BRAZIL

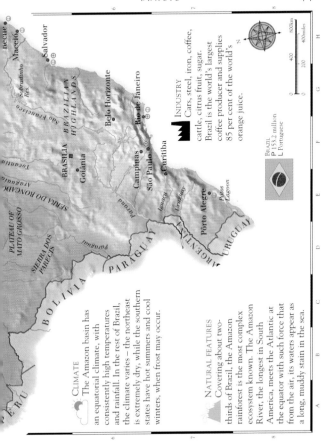

CLIMATE

The Amazon basin has an equatorial climate, with consistently high temperatures and rainfall. In the rest of Brazil, the climate varies – the northeast is extremely dry, while the southern states have hot summers and cool winters, when frost may occur.

NATURAL FEATURES

Covering about two-thirds of Brazil, the Amazon rainforest is the most complex ecosystem known. The Amazon River, the longest in South America, meets the Atlantic at the equator with such force that from the air, its waters appear as a long, muddy stain in the sea.

INDUSTRY

Cars, steel, iron, coffee, cattle, citrus fruit, sugar. Brazil is the world's largest coffee producer and supplies 85 per cent of the world's orange juice.

BRAZIL
P 153.2 million
L Portuguese

SOUTHERN SOUTH AMERICA

THE LANDSCAPE OF this region of South America varies from snow-capped volcanoes in the Andes to the wastelands of Patagonia. In the heart of Argentina lie the Pampas, fertile grasslands where vast herds of cattle graze. In parts, grasses grow up to 3 m (10 ft) high. Chile is separated from the rest of the region by the Andes, which run the length of the continent.

CLIMATE
Paraguay is subtropical; farther south is temperate. The Andes have year-round snow, while parts of the Atacama desert in Chile have had no rain for 400 years.

URUGUAY
P 3.1 million
L Spanish

PARAGUAY
P 5 million
L Spanish,
Guaraní

BRAZIL

Apa

PARAGUAY

Ciudad
del Este

Paraguay

ASUNCIÓN

Pilcomayo

Paraná

Pilcomayo

Corrientes

Bermejo

Formosa

Resistencia

Salado

GRAN CHACO

L. Mar
Chiquita

San Miguel
de Tucumán

Santiago
del Estero

Salta

Córdoba

San Salvador
de Jujuy

B O L I V I A

A N D E S

C H I L E

ATACAMA DESERT

Copiapó

La Serena

PERU

Arica

PACIFIC OCEAN

INDUSTRY
Copper, wool, beef, wheat. Chile is the world's largest copper producer, and Uruguay is the second-largest wool exporter.

ARGENTINA
P 33.1 million
L Spanish

HISTORY
Before the discovery of Cape Horn at the tip of the continent in 1616, ships used the dangerous Straits of Magellan to travel between the Atlantic and the Pacific Oceans. Today, ships use the Panama Canal.

NATURAL FEATURES
The longest chain of mountains in the world, the Andes extend for 7,240 km (4,500 miles). They are the most recently formed mountains on Earth, and the area suffers from earthquakes and volcanic activity. Glaciers, fjords, lakes, and deep-cut channels are features of the southern Andes.

ATLANTIC OCEAN

MONTEVIDEO

Río Cuarto
BUENOS AIRES
Mar del Plata
Bahía Blanca
Colorado
Negro
Gulf of San Matías
Valdés Peninsula
Comodoro Rivadavia
Deseado
Puerto Santa Cruz
Strait of Magellan
Cape Horn
TIERRA DEL FUEGO
Punta Arenas

P A M P A S
L O S   A N D E S
P A T A G O N I A

Mendoza
Godoy Cruz
SANTIAGO
San Bernardo
Viña del Mar
Valparaíso
Chillán
Concepción
Talcahuano
Los Ángeles
Temuco
Valdivia
Osorno
Puerto Montt
Chiloé I.

Bío Bío
L. Nahuel Huapi
L. Colhué Huapi
Chubut
San Carlos de Bariloche
L. Buenos Aires
L. Viedma
L. Argentino
TORRES DEL PAINE

C H I L E

CHILE
P 13.6 million
L Spanish

0   300   600 km
0   150   300 miles

THE ANTARCTIC

CONTAINING 80 PER CENT of the world's fresh water, the continent of Antarctica lies buried under ice more than 2 km (1.2 miles) thick. The surrounding seas are partly frozen, and icebergs barricade over 90 per cent of the coastline.

ATLANTIC OCEAN

INDIAN OCEAN

South Orkney Is. (to U.K.)

SCOTIA SEA

Drake Passage

Elephant I. (to U.K.)

South Shetland Is. (to U.K.)

ANTARCTIC PENINSULA

WEDDELL SEA

Anvers I. (to U.S.A.)

QUEEN MAUD LAND

Lützow-Holm Bay

ENDERBY LAND

C. Darnley

Mackenzie Bay

PALMER LAND

SOUTH POLAR PLATEAU

BELLINGSHAUSEN SEA

ELLSWORTH MTS.

·South Pole

TRANSANTARCTIC MTS.

Peter the First I. (to Norway)

DAVIS SEA

MARIE BYRD LAND

AMUNDSEN SEA

Vincennes Bay

PACIFIC OCEAN

C. Colbeck

ROSS SEA

WILKES LAND

Porpoise Bay

C. Adare

Balleny Is.

FLORA AND FAUNA

Not many plants and animals can survive on land, although the surrounding seas teem with life. Despite the cold, few birds and sea creatures migrate to warmer waters.

CLIMATE

Powerful winds form a narrow storm belt that creates severe blizzards. Summer temperatures barely reach over freezing point, and in winter the temperature can fall to –80°C (–112°F).

ENVIRONMENT

Scientists estimate that the ozone hole emerged over Antarctica in 1980. Each spring, increased sunshine activates CFCs, leading to rapid ozone depletion.

THE ARCTIC

A FROZEN OCEAN surrounded by land, the Arctic is covered by ice up to 30 m (98 ft) thick. Most of the surrounding tundra, or vast treeless plains, are permanently frozen.

RUSSIAN FEDERATION

ALASKA (U.S.A.)

CHUKCHI SEA

Pevek

Wrangel I. (to Russian Fed.)

EAST SIBERIAN SEA

BEAUFORT SEA

Prudhoe Bay

Limit of Permanent Pack Ice

New Siberian Is. (to Russian Fed.)

LAPTEV SEA

Tiksi

Banks I. (to Canada)

ARCTIC OCEAN

TAIMYR PENINSULA

Melville I. (to Canada)

CANADA

Queen Elizabeth Islands

Resolute

Axel Heiberg I. (to Canada)

Limit of Permanent Pack Ice

North Pole

Severnaya Zemlya (to Russian Fed.)

KARA SEA

Devon I. (to Canada)

Ellesmere I. (to Canada)

Thule

Franz Josef Land (to Russian Fed.)

Limit of Permanent Pack Ice

Baffin I. (to Canada)

KNUD RASMUSSEN LAND

BARENTS SEA

Baffin Bay

GREENLAND (to Denmark)

SVALBARD (to Norway)

LONGYEARBYEN

Davis Strait

Godhavn

GREENLAND SEA

Spitsbergen

GODTHÅB (NUUK)

Scoresbysund

Narsarsuaq

Jan Mayen (to Norway)

ATLANTIC OCEAN

Denmark Strait

C. Farvel

ICELAND

PEOPLE
Inuits have lived in the Arctic Circle since 2500 B.C. Vikings arrived in A.D. 986.

ATLANTIC OCEAN

BENEATH THE WATERS OF the Atlantic Ocean lies the Mid-Atlantic Ridge, one of the world's longest mountain chains. Some of its peaks are so high they form islands, such as the Azores. Apart from a wide rift-valley in the centre of the ridge, the ocean consists of vast featureless plains and is 8 km (5 miles) at its deepest point.

ICELAND
P 270,000
L Icelandic

CAPE VERDE
P 340,000
L Portuguese

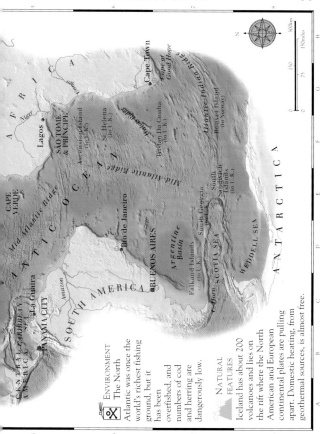

ENVIRONMENT
The North
Atlantic was once the
world's richest fishing
ground, but it
has been
overfished, and
numbers of cod
and herring are
dangerously low.

NATURAL
FEATURES
Iceland has about 200
volcanoes and lies on
the rift where the North
American and European
continental plates are pulling
apart. Domestic heating, from
geothermal sources, is almost free.

EUROPE

Jan Mayen I.
(to Norway)

NORWEGIAN SEA

ICELAND

Faeroe Islands
(to Denmark)

NORWAY

SWEDEN

EUROPE

The Alps and the Pyrenees roughly divide the continent into north and south, forming a barrier that protects warm southern countries, such as Spain and Italy, from cold northern winds. Parts of Europe are moderated by the Gulf Stream, which circulates warm waters from the Caribbean, and even seas in the Arctic Circle stay ice-free in winter.

UNITED KINGDOM

NORTH SEA

DENMARK

REPUBLIC OF IRELAND

GERMANY

CZECH REP.

1

2

3

4

AUSTR

FRANCE

5

9

ITALY

6

7

8

PORTUGAL

SPAIN

Gibraltar
(to UK)

MALTA

MEDITER

BARENTS SEA

FINLAND

BALTIC SEA
ESTONIA
LATVIA
LITHUANIA

RUSSIAN
FEDERATION

BELORUSSIA

POLAND

SLOVAKIA

HUNGARY

UKRAINE

ROMANIA

12

15

13

BULGARIA

14

BLACK SEA

GEORGIA

AZERBAIJAN
ARMENIA

GREECE

ANEAN SEA

1 NETHERLANDS
2 BELGIUM
3 LUXEMBOURG
4 LIECHTENSTEIN
5 SWITZERLAND
6 ANDORRA
7 MONACO
8 VATICAN CITY
9 SAN MARINO
10 SLOVENIA
11 CROATIA
12 BOSNIA/HERZEGOVINA
13 YUGOSLAVIA
14 MACEDONIA
15 ALBANIA
16 MOLDAVIA

SCANDINAVIA AND FINLAND

DURING PAST ICE AGES, much of Scandinavia and Finland were covered in glaciers that carved out the land, leaving steep-sided valleys, fjords, and lakes. The Finnish, originally from the east via Russia, differ from Scandinavians in culture and language.

CLIMATE
Norway's west coast is warmed by the Gulf Stream. Northern temperatures fall to –30°C (–22°F) during the six-month winter; the south is milder.

INDUSTRY
Fishing, timber, wood-pulp, paper, oil, gas, car manufacture. Norway is western Europe's largest producer of oil.

NORWAY
P 4.3 million
L Norwegian

FINLAND
P 5 million
L Finnish,
Swedish

RUSSIAN FEDERATION

ARCTIC OCEAN

North Cape

Hammerfest

Tromsø

FINLAND

Inari

Ounas

Muonio

Torne

L.Uddjaur

Kalix

Lule

Ume

Oulu

L. Oulu

North Cape

NORWEGIAN SEA

Lofoten Islands

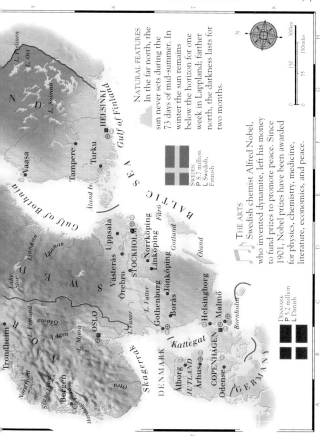

NATURAL FEATURES
In the far north, the sun never sets during the 73 days of mid-summer. In winter the sun remains below the horizon for one week in Lapland; farther north, the darkness lasts for two months.

SWEDEN
P 8.7 million
L Swedish, Finnish

THE ARTS
Swedish chemist, Alfred Nobel, who invented dynamite, left his money to fund prizes to promote peace. Since 1901, Nobel prizes have been awarded for physics, chemistry, medicine, literature, economics, and peace.

DENMARK
P 5.2 million
L Danish

N

0   75   150miles
0   150   300km

L. Paijanne
L. Ori
HELSINKI
L. Saimaa
Gulf of Finland
Vaasa
Tampere
Turku
Åland Is.
BALTIC SEA
Gulf of Bothnia
Uppsala
Ljungan
Ljusnan
Lake Stor
L. Vaner
STOCKHOLM
Norrköping
Linköping
Fårö
Gotland
Västerås
Örebro
L. Vaner
L. Vätter
Öland
Trondheim
Lake Fæmund
L. Mussa
Lågen
OSLO
Gothenburg
Borås
Jönköping
Bornholm
Norefjord
Siljan
Bergen
Otra
Skagerrak
Kattegat
Helsingborg
Malmö
DENMARK
Ålborg
JUTLAND
Århus
Odense
COPENHAGEN
GERMANY

THE BRITISH ISLES

LYING OFF THE COAST of mainland Europe, the British Isles consist of two main islands, Ireland and Great Britain, and many smaller islands. England, Scotland, Wales, and Northern Ireland form the United Kingdom (U.K.). The Republic of Ireland became independent of the U.K. in 1921.

NATURAL FEATURES
The highest point in the British Isles is Ben Nevis in Scotland at a height of 1,343 m (4,406 ft.).

UNITED KINGDOM
P 58 million
L English

NORTH SEA

ATLANTIC OCEAN

Shetland Is.

Orkney Is.

Aberdeen

HIGHLANDS

GRAMPIAN MTS.

SCOTLAND

Loch Ness

Loch Tay

Loch Lomond

Edinburgh

Glasgow

Arran

SOUTHERN UPLANDS

Lewis

Skye

North Uist

South Uist

Barra

Tiree

Coll

Mull

Colonsay

Jura

Islay

Kintyre

Outer Hebrides

Londonderry

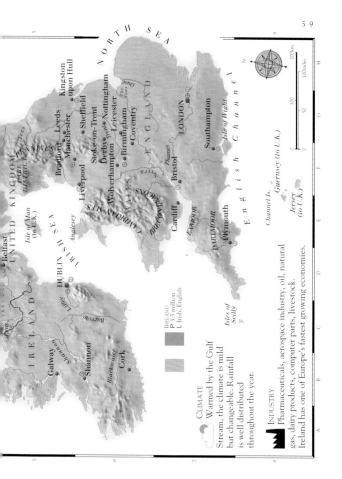

NORTH SEA

Kingston
upon Hull

Leeds

Bradford   Tees

Manchester

Sheffield

PENNINES

PEAK
DISTRICT

UNITED KINGDOM

Isle of Man
(to U.K.)

Liverpool

Nottingham

Stoke-on-Trent

Derby   Trent   Leicester

Birmingham

Wolverhampton   Coventry

ENGLAND

Anglesey

CAMBRIAN MTS.

WALES

BRECON BEACONS

Severn

Thames

Bristol

LONDON

Southampton

Isle of Wight

Cardiff

EXMOOR

DARTMOOR

Plymouth

English Channel

Channel Is.

Guernsey (to U.K.)

Jersey
(to U.K.)

Belfast

N. IRELAND (U.K.)

IRISH SEA

DUBLIN

Liffey

IRELAND

Galway

Shannon

Shannon

Blackwater

Cork

Barrow

Suir

IRELAND
P 3.5 million
L Irish, English

Isles of
Scilly

CLIMATE
Warmed by the Gulf
Stream, the climate is mild
but changeable. Rainfall
is well distributed
throughout the year.

INDUSTRY
Pharmaceuticals, aerospace industry, oil, natural
gas, dairy products, computer parts, livestock.
Ireland has one of Europe's fastest growing economies.

N

0   100   200 km

0   50   100 miles

SPAIN AND PORTUGAL

SUPREME SKILL IN shipbuilding and navigation enabled both Spain and Portugal to become the most powerful empires of the 16th century. Both have a seafaring history; Christopher Columbus sailed to America in 1492, and Vasco da Gama, the Portuguese explorer, was the first to sail around Africa to India in 1497.

INDUSTRY
Fishing, car manufacture, olives, cork, ship building, citrus fruit, tourism. Spain and Portugal are famous for fortified wines. Sherry is named after Jerez de la Frontera, Spain, and Port after Porto, Portugal.

CLIMATE
Spain's coastal areas are milder than the central plateau, which has a more extreme temperature range. Almeria, Spain, contains Europe's only desert. Portugal's Mediterranean climate is moderated by the Atlantic.

ATLANTIC OCEAN

Oviedo

Santiago de Compostela

Galicia

Minho

Esla Res.

Porto

Douro

Coimbra

Tagus

Alcántara Res.

LISBON

Setúbal

PORTUGAL

Guadiana

Beja

SIERRA

Sevilla

Lagos

Faro

PORTUGAL
P 9.9 million
L Portuguese

Gibraltar
GIBRALTAR
(to U.K.)

Strait of

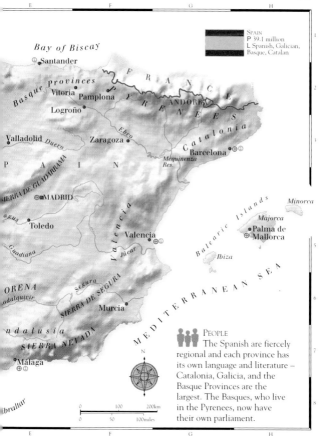

E   F   G   H

1

SPAIN
P 39.1 million
L Spanish, Galician,
Basque, Catalan

Bay of Biscay
⊕ Santander

F R A N C E

Basque Provinces
Vitoria Pamplona
2

Logroño

P Y R E N E E S

ANDORRA

Valladolid *Duero* Zaragoza ● *Ebro*

Catalonia

Barcelona ●⊕⊞
3

*Mequinenza
Res.*

SIERRA DE GUADARRAMA

⊞■ MADRID

P   A   I   N

agus

Toledo ●

Guadiana

Valencia

Valencia ●
⊕⊞

Júcar

Balearic Islands

Minorca

Majorca

● Palma de
Mallorca
5

Ibiza

ORENA

adalquivir

Segura

SIERRA DE SEGURA

Murcia ●

M E D I T E R R A N E A N   S E A
6

ndalusia

SIERRA NEVADA

● Málaga
⊕

N

braltar

0   100   200km
0   50   100miles

PEOPLE
The Spanish are fiercely
regional and each province has
its own language and literature –
Catalonia, Galicia, and the
Basque Provinces are the
largest. The Basques, who live
in the Pyrenees, now have
their own parliament.

E   F   G   H
8

FRANCE

FOLLOWING THE FRENCH Revolution (1789–99), France became Europe's first modern republic, and possessed a colonial empire that included parts of Asia and Africa. France and Spain jointly governed Andorra from 1278. In 1993 the principality held its first full elections. The country of Monaco is a lucrative banking centre.

English Channel

Cherbourg
Le Havre
Channel Islands (to U.K.)
Caen
NORMANDY

Île d'Ouessant
Brest
BRITTANY
Rennes
Le Mans

Belle Île
Loire
Nantes

ATLANTIC

Poitie

PEOPLE
Despite a strong national identity, the Bretons, Normans, Alsatians, Corsicans, and the Monegasque from Monaco still maintain their regional traditions.

ANDORRA
P 59,000
L Catalan

Bordeaux
Garonn

OCEAN

N

0   75   150km
0   50   100miles

COMMUNICATIONS
The French lead the world in high-speed train technology. First run in 1981, the TGV (*Train à Grande Vitesse*) is one of the world's fastest trains, with a top speed of 300 km/h (186 mph).

PYRENEE

SPAIN

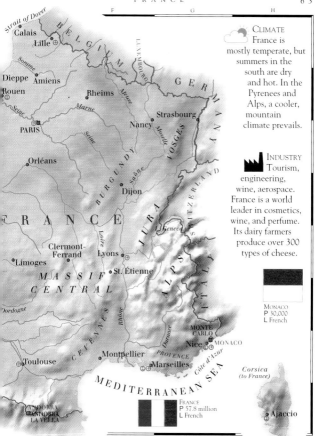

F G H

CLIMATE
France is mostly temperate, but summers in the south are dry and hot. In the Pyrenees and Alps, a cooler, mountain climate prevails.

INDUSTRY
Tourism, engineering, wine, aerospace. France is a world leader in cosmetics, wine, and perfume. Its dairy farmers produce over 300 types of cheese.

MONACO
P 30,000
L French

FRANCE
P 57.8 million
L French

Strait of Dover
Calais
Lille

BELGIUM
LUXEMBOURG
GERMANY

Somme
Dieppe Amiens
Rouen
Seine
Rheims
Marne
Strasbourg
Nancy
Moselle
PARIS
Seine
VOSGES

Orléans
BURGUNDY
Loire
Saône
Dijon
JURA
SWITZERLAND
L. Geneva

FRANCE
Clermont-Ferrand
Lyons
Limoges
St. Étienne
MASSIF CENTRAL
ALPS
ITALY
Dordogne
Rhône
CÉVENNES
MONTE CARLO
Nice MONACO
Durance
Toulouse
Montpellier
PROVENCE
Marseilles
Côte d'Azur

ANDORRA
ANDORRA LA VELLA

MEDITERRANEAN SEA

Corsica (to France)
Ajaccio

F G

THE LOW COUNTRIES

BELGIUM, THE NETHERLANDS, and Luxembourg are known as the "Low Countries" because they are flat and low-lying. Much of the Netherlands lies below sea level and has been reclaimed from the sea. The Low Countries, also called "Benelux", are Europe's most densely populated countries.

CLIMATE
The region is mostly temperate. Coastal areas are mildest, warmed by the Gulf Stream. Luxembourg's winters are cold and snowy.

NETHERLANDS
P 15.2 million
L Dutch

GERMANY

Groningen
Assen
Leeuwarden
Waddenzee
West Frisian Is.
Zwolle
Flevoland
Enschede
Apeldoorn
Arnhem
Rhine
Ijsselmeer
AMSTERDAM
Haarlem
Utrecht
Nijmegen
The Hague
Rotterdam
Dordrecht
's-Hertogenbosch
Breda
Bergen op Zoom
Eindhoven
Middelburg
NORTH SEA

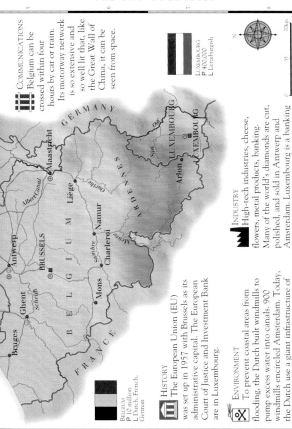

COMMUNICATIONS

Belgium can be crossed within four hours by car or train. Its motorway network is so extensive and so well lit that, like the Great Wall of China, it can be seen from space.

LUXEMBOURG
P 400,000
L Letzeburgish

N

20km
40miles

HISTORY

The European Union (EU) was set up in 1957 with Brussels as its administrative capital. The European Court of Justice and Investment Bank are in Luxembourg.

INDUSTRY

High-tech industries, cheese, flowers, metal products, banking. Many of the world's diamonds are cut, polished, and sold in Antwerp and Amsterdam. Luxembourg is a banking centre and tax haven.

ENVIRONMENT

To prevent coastal areas from flooding, the Dutch built windmills to pump excess water into canals. 900 windmills encircled Amsterdam. Today, the Dutch use a giant infrastructure of canals, dykes, and dunes.

BELGIUM
P 10 million
L Dutch, French, German

GERMANY

IT WAS NOT UNTIL 1871 that many small independent states were united under Prussia to form Germany. After 1945, the country was divided again, into a democratic West Germany and a Soviet-dominated East Germany. Reunified in 1990, Germany is, with France, a leading member of the European Union and is currently Europe's strongest economic power.

INDUSTRY
Cars, heavy and precision engineering, electronics, chemicals. Germany has a strong industrial sector and is Europe's main car producer.

POLAND

Rügen

BERLIN

Potsdam

BALTIC SEA

Mecklenburg Bay

Rostock

L. Müritz

Elbe

Kiel

Lübeck

Schwerin

Magdeburg

DENMARK

Kiel Canal

Hamburg

SAXONY

Brunswick

Mittelland Canal

Elbe

HARZ MTS.

North Frisian Is.

Bremen

Hanover

Weser

Bielefeld

East Frisian Is.

Holstein

NORTH SEA

Dortmund-Ems Canal

Ems

Münster

Dortmund

NETHERLANDS

Essen

Duisburg

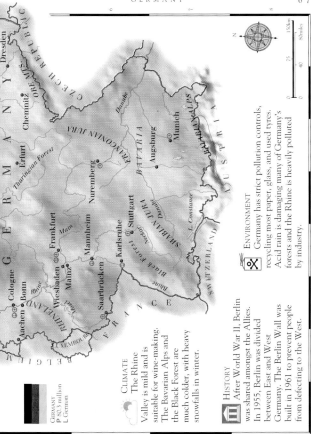

CLIMATE
The Rhine Valley is mild and is suitable for wine-making. The Bavarian Alps and the Black Forest are much colder, with heavy snowfalls in winter.

HISTORY
After World War II, Berlin was shared amongst the Allies. In 1955, Berlin was divided between East and West Germany. The Berlin Wall was built in 1961 to prevent people from defecting to the West.

ENVIRONMENT
Germany has strict pollution controls, recycling most paper, glass, and used tyres. Acid rain is damaging many of Germany's forests and the Rhine is heavily polluted by industry.

GERMANY
P 80.3 million
L German

Switzerland and Austria

Once the centre of the vast Hapsburg Empire, Austria became an independent country in 1918. Switzerland has been a neutral country since 1815, and many international organizations, such as the Red Cross, have their headquarters there. Liechtenstein is closely allied to Switzerland, which handles its foreign relations.

LIECHTENSTEIN
P 30,000
L German

SWITZERLAND
P 6.9 million
L German,
French, Italian

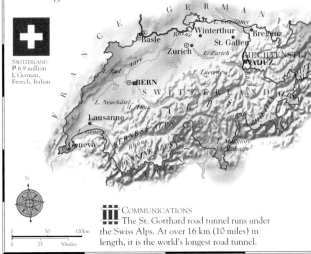

COMMUNICATIONS
The St. Gotthard road tunnel runs under the Swiss Alps. At over 16 km (10 miles) in length, it is the world's longest road tunnel.

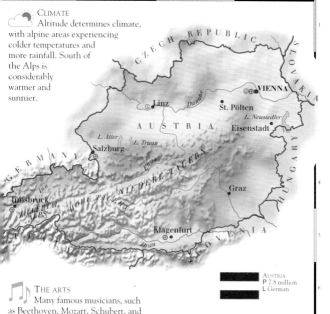

CLIMATE
Altitude determines climate, with alpine areas experiencing colder temperatures and more rainfall. South of the Alps is considerably warmer and sunnier.

THE ARTS
Many famous musicians, such as Beethoven, Mozart, Schubert, and Brahms, lived and worked in Vienna.

NATURAL FEATURES
The Alps form part of an almost continuous mountain-belt, stretching from the Pyrenees in France to the Himalayas in Asia. They are also the source of Europe's largest rivers – the Rhine, Rhône, and Danube.

AUSTRIA
P 7.8 million
L German

INDUSTRY
Pharmaceuticals, financial services, tourism, chemicals, electrical engineering. Liechtenstein is the centre of world dental manufacture. False teeth and dental materials are exported to over 100 countries.

CENTRAL EUROPE

HISTORICALLY ONE OF the least stable parts of the continent, central Europe became part of the Eastern Bloc after World War II. Czechoslovakia, Poland, and Hungary all had communist governments with strong ties with the former U.S.S.R. In 1989, they broke away from communism and in 1993 Czechoslovakia split into the Czech Republic and Slovakia.

POLAND
P 38.4 million
L Polish

CZECH REPUBLIC
P 10.3 million
L Czech

BELORUSSIA

LITHUANIA

RUSSIAN FEDERATION
KALININGRAD OBLAST

PODLASIE

L. Mamry

L. Śniardwy

Krzna

Lublin

Narew

Bug

WARSAW

Vistula

L. Jeziorak

Łódź

BALTIC SEA

Gdańsk

Bydgoszcz

L. Włocławskie

Warta

POLAND

Wisła

Poznań

Prosna

Wrocław

Odra

Warta

Odra

Pomeranian Bay

POMERANIA

Noteć

SILE

GERMANY

HUNGARY
P 10.5 million
L Hungarian
(Magyar)

SLOVAKIA
P 5.3 million
L Slovak

CLIMATE

Central Europe has a continental climate, with wet springs, late summers, and cold winters. Snow can cover eastern Poland for almost three months.

INDUSTRY

Wood industries, coal, sulphur, iron, steel, copper, fruit, spa resorts. Hungary's flat plains are among the most fertile in Europe. Slovakia and the Czech Republic have large timber industries.

ENVIRONMENT

After 1945, the central European states industrialized rapidly. Today, only four per cent of Poland's rivers have water fit for consumption, and half of its cities have no sewage treatment facilities.

ITALY AND MALTA

THE BOOT-SHAPED PENINSULA of Italy stretches from the Alps to the Ionian Sea and includes Sardinia, Sicily, and other small, offshore islands. Italy also contains two independent enclaves – the Vatican City in Rome and the Republic of San Marino near Rimini. The Romans, Arabs, French, Turks, Spanish, and British have all fought for or colonized Malta, which has been independent since 1964.

PEOPLE

The Venetians were a seafaring people, whose ships carried silks and spices from Asia. The Venetian trader and explorer Marco Polo is said to have brought the recipe for pasta from China.

HISTORY

Italy was once a collection of small kingdoms and city-states, which were vulnerable to internal wars. It was united in 1870, through the efforts of the soldier Giuseppe Garibaldi and the politician Count Camillo di Cavour.

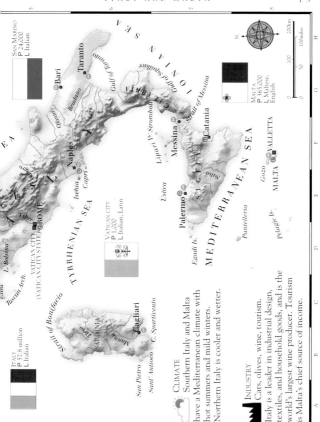

ITALY
P 57.8 million
L Italian

SAN MARINO
P 24,000
L Italian

VATICAN CITY
P 1,000
L Italian, Latin

MALTA
P 365,000
L Maltese,
English

ADRIATIC SEA

Taranto

Bari

Ofanto

Bradano

Gulf of Taranto

Gulf of Squillace

C A L A B R I A

IONIAN SEA

Strait of Messina

Catania

Messina

Lipari I.▲ Stromboli

Lipari Is.

S I C I L Y

Salso

Palermo

Ustica

Egadi Is.

Pantelleria

Pelagie Is.

Gozo

MALTA ⦿ VALLETTA

MEDITERRANEAN SEA

TYRRHENIAN SEA

Naples

Ischia

Capri

VATICAN CITY
(VATICAN CITY STATE) ⦿ ROME

Tiber

L. Bolsena

Tuscan Arch.

SEA

San Pietro

Sant' Antioco

C. Spartivento

Mannu

Tirso

SARDINIA

Cagliari

Strait of Bonifacio

N
200km
100 miles
0 50 100

☁ **CLIMATE**
Southern Italy and Malta
have a Mediterranean climate with
hot summers and mild winters.
Northern Italy is cooler and wetter.

🏭 **INDUSTRY**
Cars, olives, wine, tourism.
Italy is a leader in industrial design,
textiles, and household goods, and is the
world's largest wine producer. Tourism
is Malta's chief source of income.

THE WESTERN BALKANS

THE COUNTRIES OF Slovenia, Croatia, Dalmatia, Serbia, Montenegro, and Bosnia and Herzegovina were first united in 1918 and were named Yugoslavia in 1929. In 1991, civil war broke out between the main ethnic groups (Serbs, Muslims, Croats) resulting in the dissolution of communist Yugoslavia in 1992. Serbia and Montenegro have since formed the Federal Republic of Yugoslavia, but warfare continues in Bosnia.

INDUSTRY
Coal, chromium, mercury ore.
UN sanctions against Yugoslavia and war in Bosnia have taken a toll on their economies.

SLOVENIA
P 2 million
L Slovene

YUGOSLAVIA
P 10.5 million
L Serbo-Croatian

ROMANIA

HUNGARY

AUSTRIA

Maribor

LJUBLJANA
SLOVENIA

ZAGREB

Karlovac

CROATIA

Sava

Osijek

Zrenjanin

Novi Sad

BELGRADE

Smederevo

Pančevo

SERBIA

Banja Luka

Prijedor

Tuzla

BOSNIA &
HERZEGOVINA

DINARIC

Cres

C. Kamenjak

ITALY

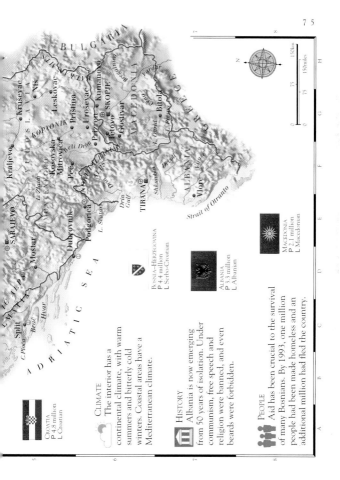

BULGARIA

N

0   75   150km
0   75   150miles

Niš
Kruševac
Kraljevo
Leskovac
KOPAONIK
Priština
Uroševac
Kumanovo
Vranje
Vardar
SKOPJE
Kosovska
Mitrovica
Peć
Tetovo
Gostivar
MACEDONIA
Beli Drim
La Zladi
MONTENEGRO
Bitola
Drim
SARAJEVO
Mostar
Podgorica
Pčinja
Dubrovnik
Crni Drim
Prespa
GREECE
Drin
Gulf
TIRANA
Shkumbin
ALBANIA
Vlorë
Vijosë
Drin
Devol
L. Scutari

ADRIATIC   SEA

Split
C. Ploča
Brač
Hvar

Strait of Otranto

CROATIA
P 4.8 million
L Croatian

CLIMATE
The interior has a continental climate, with warm summers and bitterly cold winters. Coastal areas have a Mediterranean climate.

BOSNIA–HERZEGOVINA
P 4.4 million
L Serbo-Croatian

ALBANIA
P 3.3 million
L Albanian

MACEDONIA
P 2.1 million
L Macedonian

HISTORY
Albania is now emerging from 50 years of isolation. Under communism, free speech and religion were banned, and even beards were forbidden.

PEOPLE
Aid has been crucial to the survival of many Bosnians. By 1993, one million people had been made homeless and an additional million had fled the country.

EUROPE

ROMANIA AND BULGARIA

AFTER A LONG history of invasion and occupation, Romania and Bulgaria became part of the Soviet bloc after World War II. In the early 1990s, Romania and Bulgaria rose up against their repressive communist governments – Bulgaria's president was imprisoned and Romania's was executed.

ROMANIA
P 23.3 million
L Romanian

UKRAINE

L. Razim

Danube Delta

Braila

Galaţi

Buzău

M O L D A V I A

Prut

Iaşi

Focşani

Siret

Piatra-Neamţ

Bacău

Botoşani

Suceava

Bistriţa

Buzău

Ploieşti

Braşov

Târgovişte

Rîmnicu Vîlcea

C A R P A T H I A N S

T R A N S Y L V A N I A N   A L P S

CARPATHIANS

Sibiu

Târgu Mureş

Baia Mare

Someş

Satu Mare

Cluj-Napoca

Mureş

R O M A N I A

U K R A I N E

Timiş

Arad

Reşiţa

H U N G A R Y

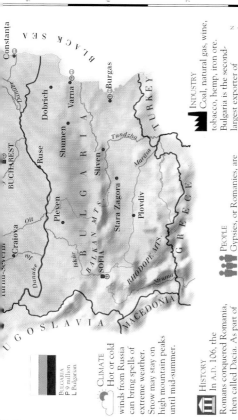

BLACK SEA

Constanța

Dobrich

Ruse

Varna

Burgas

Shumen

BUCHAREST

Danube

Craiova

Pleven

Sliven

TURKEY

Tundzha

Olt

B U L G A R I A

Iskŭr

Maritsa

SOFIA

Stara Zagora

Plovdiv

Olt

Danube

BALKAN Mts.

RHODOPE Mts.

G R E E C E

Struma

MACEDONIA

YUGOSLAVIA

BULGARIA
P 9 million
L Bulgarian

CLIMATE

Hot or cold winds from Russia can bring spells of extreme weather. Snow may stay on high mountain peaks until mid-summer.

HISTORY

In A.D. 106, the Romans conquered Romania, then called Dacia. As part of the Roman Empire, Dacians adopted Roman customs as well as the Latin language. The modern language of Romanian developed from spoken Latin.

INDUSTRY

Coal, natural gas, wine, tobacco, hemp, iron ore. Bulgaria is the second-largest exporter of cigarettes and supplies most of the world's rose oil, used in perfume.

N

150km

75

0

80miles

40

PEOPLE

Gypsies, or Romanies, are thought to have come from India, via the Middle East, during the 5th century. They claimed to have come from a country called Little Egypt – "Gypsy" is derived from the word "Egyptian".

GREECE

SURROUNDED BY THE Aegean, Ionian, and Cretan seas, no part of Greece is more than 137 km (85 miles) from the coast. Its territory includes the mainland on the Balkan peninsula, and more than 1,400 islands. The country is mountainous and less than one-third of the land is cultivated. Greece gained its independence in 1830 after a long and fierce war, ending 400 years of Turkish rule.

L. Prespa
ALBANIA
Aliakmon
Corfu
Corfu
PINDUS MTS.
IONIAN IS.
IONIAN SEA
Levkas
Akheloos
L. Trikhonis
Kefallinia
Gulf of Patrai
Zakinthos

GREECE
P 10.3 million
L Greek

CLIMATE

Northwestern Greece is alpine, while parts of Crete are almost subtropical. The islands and the large central plain of the mainland have a Mediterranean climate, with high summer temperatures and mild winters.

ENVIRONMENT

Athens suffers from smog, known as *nefos*, which damages its ancient monuments. The Parthenon, part of the Acropolis, has suffered more erosion in the previous two decades than in the past two thousand years.

HISTORY

Regarded as the founders of democracy, the ancient Greeks were advanced for their time. They were the first to study medicine, geometry, and physics (on a scientific basis), and Greece was home to great thinkers such as Plato, Aristotle, and Socrates.

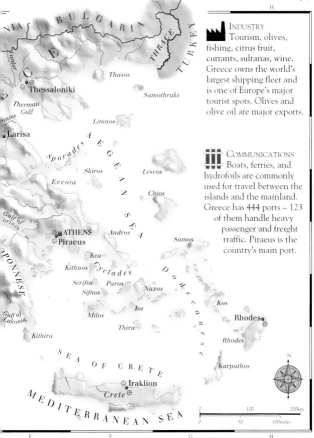

INDUSTRY
Tourism, olives, fishing, citrus fruit, currants, sultanas, wine. Greece owns the world's largest shipping fleet and is one of Europe's major tourist spots. Olives and olive oil are major exports.

COMMUNICATIONS
Boats, ferries, and hydrofoils are commonly used for travel between the islands and the mainland. Greece has 444 ports – 123 of them handle heavy passenger and freight traffic. Piraeus is the country's main port.

Map labels:

BULGARIA

THRACE

TURKEY

Thasos

Thessaloniki

Samothraki

Thermaic Gulf

Limnos

Larisa

Sporades

A E G E A N   S E A

Skiros

Lesvos

Evvoia

Chios

Gulf of Corinth

ATHENS
Piraeus

Andros

Samos

PELOPONNESE

Kea

Kithnos

Cyclades

Dodecanese

Serifos   Paros

Sifnos   Naxos

Gulf of Lakonia

Ios

Kos

Milos

Thira

Rhodes

Kithira

Rhodes

S E A   O F   C R E T E

Karpathos

Iraklion

Crete

M E D I T E R R A N E A N   S E A

N

0   100   200km

0   50   100miles

THE BALTIC STATES AND BELORUSSIA

LITHUANIA, ESTONIA, AND LATVIA – the three Baltic States – were the first republics to declare their independence from the Soviet Union in 1990-91. Economic reform has been slow and problems such as food shortages still remain. Many areas of Belorussia are still affected by the 1986 Chernobyl nuclear disaster. The clean-up will take decades, and is a major drain on the nation's finances.

PEOPLE
Russians, Belorussians, and Ukrainians resettled in Latvia when it was part of the U.S.S.R. Today Latvians make up only about half of the whole population, and they are a minority in the capital.

ESTONIA
P 1.6 million
L Estonian

LATVIA
P 2.7 million
L Latvian

BELORUSSIA
P 10.3 million
L Belorussian

LITHUANIA
P 3.8 million
L Lithuanian

RUSSIA

Gulf of Finland

Narva

ESTONIA

TALLINN

L. Peipus

Tartu

Pärnu

Võrtsjärv

Hiiumaa

Saaremaa

Gulf of Riga

RIGA

Venta

Liepāja

BALTIC

LITHUANIA

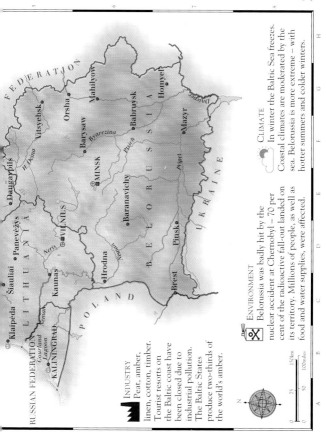

FEDERATION

Daugavpils • Vitsyebsk • Orsha • Mahilyow

Šiauliai • Panevėžys Barysaw • Byarezina • Babruysk • Homyel

LITHUANIA VILNIUS MINSK Dnieper

Klaipėda Nemar Neris Baranavichy Mazyr Pripet

Kaunas Hrodna Uman BELORUSSIA Pripet

Courland Lagoon POLAND Pinsk • Brest UKRAINE

RUSSIAN FEDERATION

KALININGRAD

INDUSTRY

Peat, amber, linen, cotton, timber. Tourist resorts on the Baltic coast have been closed due to industrial pollution. The Baltic States produce two-thirds of the world's amber.

ENVIRONMENT

Belorussia was badly hit by the nuclear accident at Chernobyl – 70 per cent of the radioactive fall-out landed on its territory. Millions of people, as well as food and water supplies, were affected.

CLIMATE

In winter the Baltic Sea freezes. Coastal climates are moderated by the sea. Belorussia is more extreme – with hotter summers and colder winters.

N

0   75   150km
0   50   100miles

EUROPEAN RUSSIA

SPANNING THE TWO continents of Europe and Asia, the Russian Federation is the world's largest country. In 1917, the world's first communist government took power and in 1923, Russia became the U.S.S.R., which included many territories that were once part of the Russian Empire. Economic reforms in the 1980s led to changes resulting in the fall of communism in 1991.

INDUSTRY
Oil, gas, gold, diamonds, hydrocarbons, precious metals. Russia has large reserves of iron, coal, and nickel. Huge factories, which have grown without environmental controls, are causing pollution problems.

KARA SEA

Novaya Zemlya

Kara Strait

Yugor Luyagach I.

Vorkuta

Uso

Pechora

BARENTS SEA

Kolguyev I.

Murmansk

L. Imandra

KOLA PENINSULA

Arkhangel'sk

WHITE SEA

L. Pyaozero

L. Topozero

L. Segozero

L. Onega

Oz.

L. Ladoga

St. Petersburg

FINLAND

RUSSIA

ESTONIA

LATVIA

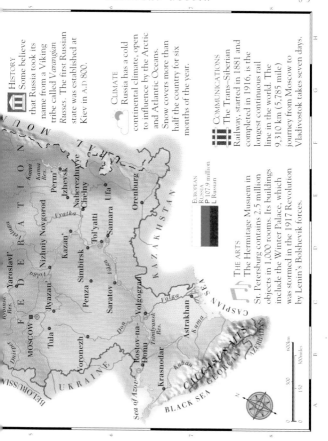

HISTORY

Some believe that Russia took its name from a Viking tribe called *Varangian Russes*. The first Russian state was established at Kiev in A.D 800.

CLIMATE

Russia has a cold continental climate, open to influence by the Arctic and Atlantic Oceans. Snow covers more than half the country for six months of the year.

COMMUNICATIONS

The Trans–Siberian Railway, started in 1881 and completed in 1916, is the longest continuous rail line in the world. The 9,310 km (5,785 mile) journey from Moscow to Vladivostok takes seven days.

THE ARTS

The Hermitage Museum in St. Petersburg contains 2.5 million objects in 1,000 rooms. Its buildings include the Winter Palace, which was stormed in the 1917 Revolution by Lenin's Bolshevik forces.

EUROPEAN RUSSIA
P 107.9 million
L Russian

Map labels:

BELORUSSIA
UKRAINE
Kuybyshev Res.
Dnepr
MOSCOW
Tula
Voronezh
Ryazan'
Penza
Saratov
Simbirsk
Kazan'
Nizhniy Novgorod
Yaroslavl'
Vyatka
Kama Res.
Kama
Perm'
Izhevsk
Naberezhnyye Chelny
Ufa
Tol'yatti
Samara
Orenburg
Volga
Don
Tsimlyansk Res.
Rostov-na-Donu
Volgograd
Krasnodar
Astrakhan
Kuban
CASPIAN SEA
Sea of Azov
BLACK SEA
CAUCASUS MTS.
GEORGIA
AZERBAIJAN
KAZAKHSTAN
FEDERATION
N

0   150   300
0   180   600km
        300mile

UKRAINE AND
THE CAUCASUS

SEPARATED FROM the Russian Federation by the Caucasus mountains, the newly independent Caucasian Republics – Armenia, Azerbaijan, and Georgia – are rich in natural resources. The Ukraine, Europe's largest country, is dominated by a flat and fertile plain.

(map showing BELORUSSIA, POLAND, SLOVAKIA, HUNGARY, ROMANIA, MOLDAVIA, UKRAINE with labels: Chernihiv, Chernobyl, Kiev Res., KIEV, Luts'k, Rivne, Zhytomyr, L'viv, Ternopil, Bila Tserkva, Khmel'nyts'kyy, Vinnytsya, Ivano-Frankivs'k, Dniester, Chernivtsi, CHISINAU, Mykolayiv, Odesa)

ENVIRONMENT
As a result of the 1986 Chernobyl nuclear disaster, 4 million Ukrainians live in radioactive areas. In 1994, reactors from the Chernobyl plant were still being used to provide nuclear power.

MOLDAVIA
P 4.4 million
L Romanian

CLIMATE
Ukraine and Moldavia have a continental climate, with distinctive seasons. Armenia, Azerbaijan, and Georgia are protected from cold air from the north by the Caucasus mountains.

N

0   150   300km
0   75   150miles

INDUSTRY
Coal, iron, cars, wine, citrus fruit, cotton, minerals. The Ukraine was known as the "breadbasket" of the Soviet Union as its steppes were extensively cultivated. Georgia's known oil reserves are as yet unexploited.

UKRAINE
P 52 million
L Ukrainian

PEOPLE
There are about 40 languages and
150 dialects spoken in the Caucasian
republics. No relationship has yet been
established between languages spoken
within the Caucasus and those outside it.

NATURAL FEATURES
The Caucasus mountains extend
for 1,200 km (750 miles). They form a
natural boundary between Europe and
Asia, and separate temperate climate
zones from warmer climate zones.

FLORA AND FAUNA
The Russian sturgeon fish
grows up to 7m (23 ft) long. Its
eggs, called caviar, are a delicacy,
but numbers of sturgeon are falling
due to polluted water.

GEORGIA
P 5.5 million
L Georgian

AZERBAIJAN
P 7.2 million
L Azerbaijani

RUSSIAN FEDERATION

Desna
Sumy •
Kharkiv •
Kremenchuk Res.
Donets
Dnipropetrovs'k •
Kryvyy Rih •   Horlivka •   Kramators'k •
Donets'k • • Makiyivka   Luhans'k •
DONBASS
Zaporizhzhya
Kakhovka Res.
Dnieper
Mariupol' •
Kherson •

SEA OF AZOV

Kerch Strait

CRIMEA

• Simferopol'
Sevastopol' •

BLACK SEA

RUSSIAN FEDERATION

CAUCASUS

GEORGIA MTS.
K'ut'aisi •   TBILISI ■⊕
Gyumri •   Vanadzor •   *Mingäçevir Res.*
ARMENIA ⊕   Gäncä •
YEREVAN ⊕
Kura
AZERBAIJAN
BAKU ⊕ ■

TURKEY

AZERBAIJAN

IRAN

CASPIAN SEA

HISTORY
With its strategic
position, the Crimean
peninsula has had a
troubled history. It was
part of Greece until 100
B.C., Turkey from 1475,
and Russia from 1783,
and was the scene of the
Crimean War in 1853-56.

ARMENIA
P 3.5 million
L Armenian

AFRICA

MEDITERRANEAN SEA

RED SEA

TUNISIA

MOROCCO

ALGERIA

LIBYA

EGYPT

SUDAN

ERITREA

DJIBOUTI

ETHIOPIA

MALI

NIGER

CHAD

CENTRAL
AFRICAN
REPUBLIC

CAMEROON

NIGERIA

BENIN

TOGO

GHANA

BURKINA

IVORY
COAST

LIBERIA

SIERRA
LEONE

GUINEA

GUINEA-BISSAU

GAMBIA

SENEGAL

MAURITANIA

WESTERN
SAHARA

Madeira
(to Portugal)

Canary Islands
(to Spain)

SEYCHELLES

COMOROS

MADAGASCAR

KENYA

UGANDA

RWANDA

BURUNDI

TANZANIA

ZAIRE

MALAWI

MOZAMBIQUE

SWAZILAND

ZAMBIA

ZIMBABWE

LESOTHO

CONGO

ANGOLA

BOTSWANA

SOUTH AFRICA

GABON

NAMIBIA

EQUATORIAL GUINEA

SAO TOME & PRINCIPE

ATLANTIC OCEAN

AFRICA

Both tropics and the equator run through Africa, the warmest of all the continents. The land around the tropics is starved of rain creating great deserts such as the Sahara and the Kalahari. In contrast, high rainfall around the equator has produced lush tropical rainforests.

NORTHWEST AFRICA

SPANNING THE continent of Africa, from the Atlantic to the Red Sea, the Sahara covers 9 million sq km (3.5 million sq miles) and is the world's largest desert. Droughts and the over-use of land for farming are causing the Sahara to spread into the Sahel (semi-arid grasslands). Italy, the U.K., Spain, and France have all had colonies in this region.

Strait of Gibraltar

Ceuta   Melilla
(to Spain) (to Spain)

Tangier

RABAT
Casablanca   Fez
M O R O C C O
Marrakesh

Agadir   M T

A T L A S   Béchar

EL AAIÚN   A   L

Dakhla

WESTERN SAHARA   MAURITANIA   M

Morocco occupied the whole of Western Sahara in 1979.

INDUSTRY
Oil, gas, phosphates, tourism, olives, dates, fruit. Morocco and Tunisia attract millions of tourists every year. They are also leading phosphate producers. Algeria and Libya have significant oil reserves.

MOROCCO
P 27 million
L Arabic

CLIMATE
Coastal areas have a temperate climate with hot, dry summers and wet winters. Mountain areas are cooler. Most areas are affected by the many different kinds of Sahara wind, such as the *sirocco*, the *chergui*, and the *chili*.

NATURAL FEATURES
The Atlas Mountains extend over 2,410 km (1,500 miles) from the Canary Islands in the Atlantic to Tunisia. Like the Alps, the Atlas Mountains were formed when the continental plates of Europe and Africa pushed together.

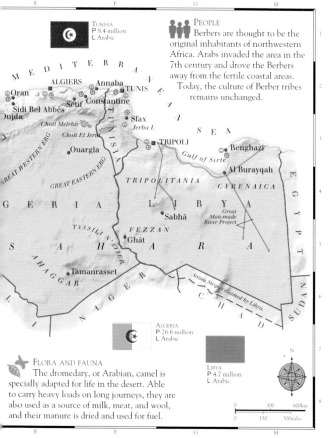

TUNISIA
P 8.4 million
L Arabic

PEOPLE
Berbers are thought to be the original inhabitants of northwestern Africa. Arabs invaded the area in the 7th century and drove the Berbers away from the fertile coastal areas. Today, the culture of Berber tribes remains unchanged.

ALGIERS Annaba
Oran TUNIS
Sidi Bel Abbès Sétif Constantine
Oujda
Chott Melrhir Sfax
Chott El Jerid Jerba I.
Ouargla TRIPOLI Benghazi
GREAT WESTERN ERG Gulf of Sirte Al Burayqah
GREAT EASTERN ERG TRIPOLITANIA CYRENAICA
ALGERIA LIBYA
TASSILI N'AJJER Sabhā Great Man-made River Project
FEZZAN
Ghāt
SAHARA
AHAGGAR
Tamanrasset
Aozou Strip is claimed by Libya

MEDITERRANEAN SEA

TUNISIA

EGYPT

NIGER CHAD SUDAN

LIBYA

ALGERIA
P 26.6 million
L Arabic

FLORA AND FAUNA
The dromedary, or Arabian, camel is specially adapted for life in the desert. Able to carry heavy loads on long journeys, they are also used as a source of milk, meat, and wool, and their manure is dried and used for fuel.

LIBYA
P 4.7 million
L Arabic

N

0 300 600km
0 150 300miles

NORTHEAST AFRICA

THE NILE, THE LONGEST river in the world, carries rich mud from the highlands of Sudan into Egypt, creating some of the most fertile land in the world. About 99 per cent of Egypt's population live on the river's banks. Ethiopia, Somalia, and Sudan have been beset by drought, famine, and war and about half of Africa's 4.5 million refugees come from this area.

EGYPT
P 56.4 million
L Arabic

HISTORY

Hieroglyphs were a set of mysterious symbols until the discovery of the Rosetta Stone in 1799. The Stone is inscribed in three different scripts: ancient Greek, demotic, and hieroglyphs. By comparing the royal names in the scripts, hieroglyphs were finally deciphered 25 years later.

ERITREA
P 3.5 million
L Tigrinya,
Arabic

MEDITERRANEAN SEA

Qattara
Depression

El Mansûra
Alexandria
Port
Saïd
CAIRO
Ismâ'ilîya
Giza
Suez
ISRAEL
Helwân
Gulf of
Aqaba
SINAI
Gulf of Suez
El Faiyûm
El Minya
Asyût
Nile
RED SEA
Sohâg
Qena
Valley of the Kings
Luxor
E G Y P T
Philae
Aswân
L. Nasser
LIBYAN DESERT
NUBIAN DESERT
Abu Simbel

L I B Y A

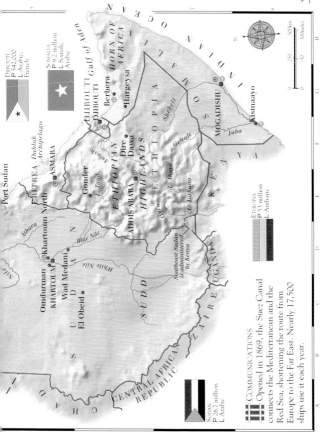

DJIBOUTI
P 542,000
L Arabic,
French

SOMALIA
P 9.2 million
L Somali,
Arabic

ETHIOPIA
P 53 million
L Amharic

SUDAN
P 26.7 million
L Arabic

INDIAN OCEAN

Gulf of Aden

HORN OF AFRICA

DJIBOUTI
Berbera
Hargeysa

DJIBOUTI

ERITREA
Dahlak Archipelago

Port Sudan

ASMARA

Gonder
L. Tana

ETHIOPIAN HIGHLANDS

Dire Dawa

Awash

ADDIS ABABA

Omo

L. Abaya

L. Turkana

SHEBELLI

Genale

Juba

MOGADISHU

Kismaayo

Khartoum North

Omdurman
KHARTOUM

Wad Medani

El Obeid

Blue Nile

White Nile

Atbara

Nile

SUDAN

SUDD

Southeast Sudan
is administered
by Kenya

CENTRAL AFRICAN REPUBLIC

CHAD

ZAIRE

UGANDA

KENYA

SOMALIA

COMMUNICATIONS
Opened in 1869, the Suez Canal connects the Mediterranean and the Red Sea, shortening the route from Europe to the Far East. Nearly 17,500 ships use it each year.

N

500km

500miles

250

150

WEST AFRICA

BY 1914, MANY European countries, such as France, Britain, and Portugal, had divided up most of Africa between them. Despite independence, foreign companies still own many of the coffee and cocoa plantations in the region.

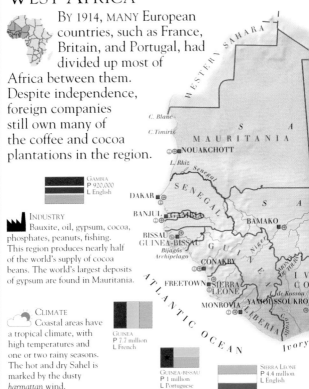

GAMBIA
P 920,000
L English

INDUSTRY
Bauxite, oil, gypsum, cocoa, phosphates, peanuts, fishing. This region produces nearly half of the world's supply of cocoa beans. The world's largest deposits of gypsum are found in Mauritania.

CLIMATE
Coastal areas have a tropical climate, with high temperatures and one or two rainy seasons. The hot and dry Sahel is marked by the dusty *harmattan* wind.

GUINEA
P 7.7 million
L French

GUINEA-BISSAU
P 1 million
L Portuguese

SIERRA LEONE
P 4.4 million
L English

WESTERN SAHARA

MAURITANIA

C. Blanc
C. Timiris
L. Rkiz
Senegal

NOUAKCHOTT

SENEGAL
DAKAR
BANJUL GAMBIA
BISSAU
GUINEA-BISSAU
Bijagós Archipelago
CONAKRY

BAMAKO

Niger

GUINEA

FREETOWN SIERRA LEONE
MONROVIA

YAMOUSSOUKRO
L. de Kossou

LIBERIA

ATLANTIC OCEAN

Ivory

S A

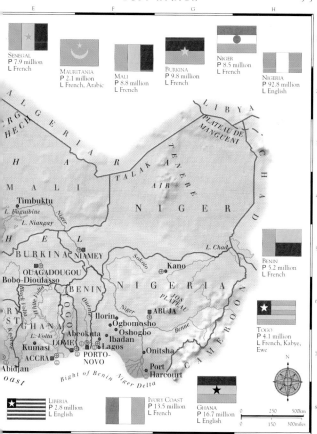

SENEGAL
P 7.9 million
L French

MAURITANIA
P 2.1 million
L French, Arabic

MALI
P 8.8 million
L French

BURKINA
P 9.8 million
L French

NIGER
P 8.5 million
L French

NIGERIA
P 92.8 million
L English

BENIN
P 5.2 million
L French

TOGO
P 4.1 million
L French, Kabye, Ewe

LIBERIA
P 2.8 million
L English

IVORY COAST
P 13.5 million
L French

GHANA
P 16.7 million
L English

A L G E R I A

HECH

L I B Y A

PLATEAU DE MANGUENI

M A L I

Timbuktu

L. Faguibine

L. Niangay

H E L

BURKINA   NIAMEY

OUAGADOUGOU

Bobo-Dioulasso

BENIN

White Volta

Black Volta

Red Volta

I V O R Y

C O A S T

G H A N A

Oti

Kainji

L. Volta

Kumasi

ACCRA

LOMÉ

PORTO-NOVO

Ilorin

Ogbomosho

Abeokuta

Oshogbo

Ibadan

Lagos

N I G E R I A

Kano

Sokoto

Niger

JOS PLATEAU

ABUJA

Benue

Onitsha

Port Harcourt

C A M E R O O N

Bight of Benin   Niger Delta

Abidjan

C o a s t

T A L A K

T É N É R É

A I R

N I G E R

L. Chad

C H A D

N

0   250   500km
0   150   300miles

CENTRAL AFRICA

MUCH OF THIS region is covered in dense tropical rainforest, drained by the Congo (Zaire) River, which forms a huge arc on its way to the Atlantic. In the 16th century Portugal and Spain set up trading posts on the west coast as part of the slave trade. Millions of Africans from this region were sent as slaves to the New World. Many people in coastal areas still speak Spanish and Portuguese.

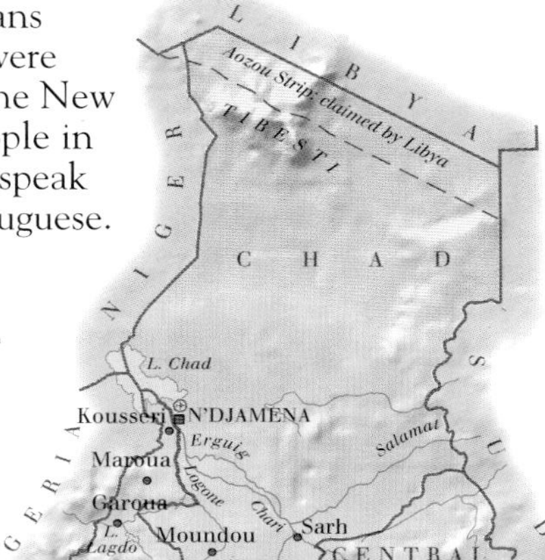

INDUSTRY
Timber, oil, iron, cocoa, coffee, copper. Bélinga, Gabon, contains the world's largest iron ore deposits. Many central African countries have unexploited oil and gas reserves.

CHAD
P 5.8 million
L French

CENTRAL AFRICAN REPUBLIC
P 3.2 million
L French

CAMEROON
P 12.2 million
L French,
English

EQUATORIAL GUINEA
P 400,000
L Spanish

Map labels: LIBYA, Aozou Strip claimed by Libya, TIBESTI, CHAD, NIGER, NIGERIA, SUDAN, CENTRAL, L. Chad, Kousséri, Kousséri, N'DJAMENA, Maroua, Verges, Garoua, Guéré, Logone, Chari, Moundou, Sarh, Jagio

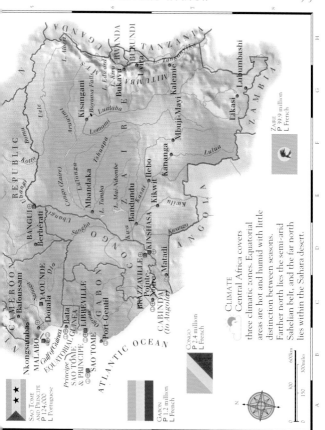

SAO TOME AND PRINCIPE
P 124,000
L Portuguese

CONGO
P 2.4 million
L French

GABON
P 1.2 million
L French

ZAIRE
P 39.9 million
L French

CLIMATE
Central Africa covers three climatic zones. Equatorial areas are hot and humid with little distinction between seasons. Farther north lies the semi-arid Sahelian belt, and the far north lies within the Sahara desert.

ATLANTIC OCEAN

0   300   600km
0   150   300miles

CENTRAL EAST AFRICA

LARGE AREAS OF savannah, or grassland, in central Africa provide grazing for both domestic and wild animals. Industry is poorly developed in the region – Zambia, Rwanda, Burundi, and Uganda suffer from having no sea ports. Lake Victoria is the largest lake in Africa, and a source of the River Nile.

FLORA AND FAUNA
Poaching remains a major problem in this area. To combat this, all the countries in this region have set up wildlife parks to protect animals such as elephants and zebra.

INDUSTRY
Tobacco, coffee, tea, tourism, cloves, copper. Zambia is the world's fifth-largest producer of copper. Wildlife parks in this region attract thousands of tourists.

RWANDA
P 7.5 million
L French,
Kinyarwanda

UGANDA
P 18.7 million
L English

KENYA
P 25.2 million
L Swahili

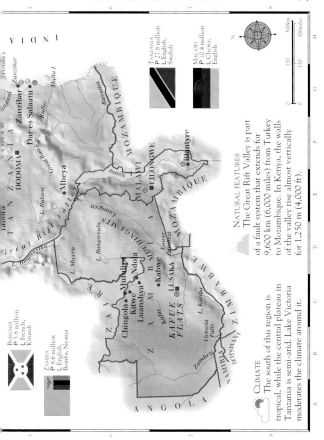

TANZANIA
P 27.8 million
L English, Swahili

MALAWI
P 10.4 million
L Chewa, English

BURUNDI
P 5.8 million
L French, Kirundi

ZAMBIA
P 8.6 million
L English, Bemba, Nyanja

N

0 | 250 | 500km
0 | 150 | 300miles

NATURAL FEATURES
The Great Rift Valley is part of a fault system that extends for 9,600 km (6,000 miles) from Turkey to Mozambique. In Kenya, the walls of the valley rise almost vertically for 1,250 m (4,000 ft).

CLIMATE
The south of this region is tropical, while the central plateau in Tanzania is semi-arid. Lake Victoria moderates the climate around it.

Map labels

INDIA

Pemba I.
Mafia I.
Zanzibar
Dar es Salaam
DODOMA
TANZANIA
Mbeya
L. Rukwa
Tabora
Ruvuma
Great Ruaha
Rufiji
Kilwa
MOZAMBIQUE
L. Tanganyika
L. Mweru
L. Bangweulu
Bangweulu
MUCHINGA MTS.
Luangwa
MALAWI
LILONGWE
Blantyre
Lower Zambezi
L. Muera
ZAIRE
Chingola
Kitwe
Mufulira
Ndola
Luanshya
Kabwe
LUSAKA
ZAMBIA
KAFUE FLATS
Kafue
Zambezi
L. Kariba
Victoria Falls
Zambezi
ZIMBABWE
NAMIBIA
BOTSWANA
ANGOLA

SOUTHERN AFRICA

THE RICHEST DEPOSITS of valuable minerals in Africa, such as gold and diamonds, are found in its southern region. Many surrounding countries rely on South Africa for work and trade. Racial segregation under apartheid operated from 1948 until 1994 when South Africa's first multi-racial elections were held. Namibia won its independence from South Africa in 1990, but neighbouring Angola has been in a state of civil war since 1975.

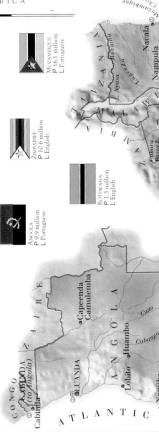

MOZAMBIQUE
P 16.1 million
L Portuguese

ZIMBABWE
P 10.6 million
L English

BOTSWANA
P 1.3 million
L English

ANGOLA
P 9.9 million
L Portuguese

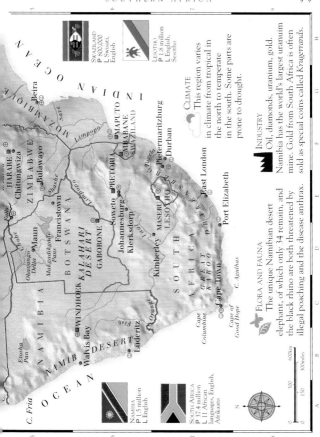

SWAZILAND
P 800,000
L Swazi, English

LESOTHO
P 1.8 million
L English, Sesotho

INDIAN OCEAN

Beira

MOZAMBIQUE

ZIMBABWE

HARARE
Chitungwiza
Bulawayo
Francistown

Sabi

Limpopo

MAPUTO
MBABANE
SWAZILAND

Save

CLIMATE
This region varies
in climate from tropical in
the north to temperate
in the south. Some parts are
prone to drought.

INDUSTRY
Oil, diamonds, uranium, gold.
Namibia has the world's largest uranium
mine. Gold from South Africa is often
sold as special coins called *Krugerrands*.

PRETORIA
Soweto
Johannesburg
Klerksdorp

Vaal

MASERU
LESOTHO

Pietermaritzburg
Durban

Tugela

East London

Port Elizabeth

GREAT KAROO

SOUTH AFRICA

Kimberley

BOTSWANA

GABORONE

KALAHARI DESERT

Makgadikgadi
Pans

Okavango
Delta

Chobe

Maun

Shashe

Okwa

NAMIBIA

WINDHOEK

Walvis Bay

Lüderitz

NAMIB DESERT

Fish

Orange

C. Fria

Etosha
Pan

OCEAN

C. Columbine

Cape of
Good Hope

Cape
Agulhas

Cape Town

FLORA AND FAUNA
The unique Namibian desert
elephant, of which only 34 remain, and
the black rhino are both threatened by
illegal poaching and the disease anthrax.

NAMIBIA
P 1.5 million
L English

SOUTH AFRICA
P 37.4 million
L 11 African
languages, English,
Afrikaans

N

0   150   300   600km
0   150   300miles

INDIAN OCEAN

THE SMALLEST of the world's oceans, the Indian Ocean has some 5,000 islands scattered across its area. Beneath its surface, three great mountain ranges converge towards the ocean's centre – an area of strong seismic and volcanic activity. The ocean's greatest depth, 7,440 m (24,400 ft), is in the Java Trench.

FLORA AND FAUNA
Owing to its position off the African coast, Madagascar is home to many unique animals, such as tenrecs, lemurs, and fossas.

ENVIRONMENT
The Indian Ocean is at risk from oil pollution from tankers carrying oil from the Persian Gulf.

CLIMATE
The monsoon winds blow over the Indian Ocean – from the southwest or from the northeast according to the season. The southwesterly monsoon brings heavy rains to southern Asia.

COMOROS
P 497,000
L Arabic,
French

MALDIVES
P 240,000
L Divehi

SEYCHELLES
P 68,000
L Creole,
English, French

Port Said
Suez
Suez Canal
Nile
Kuwait City
Persian Gulf
Karachi
Indus
Gulf of Aden
Aden
Djibouti
RED SEA
ARABIAN
ARABIAN SEA
Socotra (to Yemen)
Laksshadweep Is (to India)
A Mahé (to India)
Bombay
Calcutta
Ganges
Madras
Cochin
MALÉ
MALDIVES
Somali Basin
Sri Lanka
Nicobar Is (to India)
Andaman Is (to India)
ANDAMAN SEA
Bay of Bengal
Irrawaddy
Rangoon
Mekong
Gulf of Thailand
SOUTH CHINA SEA

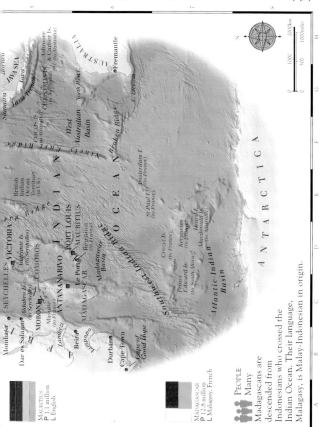

Sumatra JAVA SEA

Java French

CHRIST.IS.

CHRISTMAS I.
(to Australia)

Ashmore
& Cartier Is.
(to Australia)

North West C.

C. Leeuwin

Fremantle

AUSTRALIA

West
Australian
Basin

Ninety East Ridge

Broken Ridge

Amsterdam I.
(to France)

St Paul I.
(to France)

British
Indian
Ocean
Territory
(to U.K.)

Kerguelen
(to France)

I   N   D   I   A   N

O   C   E   A   N

A   N   T   A   R   C   T   I   C   A

SEYCHELLES   VICTORIA

Aldabra Is.
(to Seychelles)

Farquhar Is.
(to Seychelles)

Mombasa

Dar es Salaam

MORONI
Mayotte
(to France)

COMOROS

ANTANANARIVO

MADAGASCAR

Le Port
Réunion
(to France)

PORT LOUIS

MAURITIUS

Mascarene Basin

Madagascar
Basin

Mid Indian Ridge

South West Indian Ridge

Prince
Edward Is.
(to South Africa)

Crozet Is.
(to France)

Heard &
Macdonald Is.
(to Australia)

Atlantic-Indian
Basin

Zambezi

Limpopo

Beira

Durban

Cape Town

Cape of
Good Hope

MAURITIUS
P 1.1 million
L English

MADAGASCAR
P 12.8 million
L Malagasy, French

PEOPLE
Many
Madagascans are
descended from
Indonesians who crossed the
Indian Ocean. Their language,
Malagasy, is Malay-Indonesian in origin.

NORTH AND WEST ASIA

BARENTS SEA

KARA SEA

RUSSIAN FEDERATION

(EUROPEAN RUSSIA)

KAZAKHSTAN

CASPIAN SEA

BLACK SEA

GEORGIA

UZBEKISTAN

KYRGYZSTAN

ARMENIA AZERBAIJAN

TURKEY

TURKMENISTAN

TAJIKISTAN

CYPRUS

LEBANON

SYRIA

IRAQ

IRAN

AFGHANISTAN

ISRAEL

JORDAN

KUWAIT

BAHRAIN QATAR

UNITED ARAB EMIRATES

RED SEA

SAUDI ARABIA

OMAN

ARABIAN SEA

YEMEN

NORTH AND WEST ASIA

Asia is the largest continent in the world, occupying nearly one-third of the world's total land area. In the south, the Arabian Peninsula is mostly hot, dry desert. In the north lie cold deserts, treeless plains called steppes, and the largest needleleaf forest in the world, which stretches from Siberia to northern Europe.

TURKEY

BRIDGING THE CONTINENTS of Europe and Asia, Turkey was once the centre of the Ottoman Empire, which controlled a quarter of Europe. Cyprus became independent from the UK in 1960, but was invaded by Turkey in 1974. Southern Cyprus is Greek; Turkish Northern Cyprus is recognized by only Turkey.

TURKEY
P 59.9 million
L Turkish

BULGARIA
GREECE

Bosporus
Istanbul
Sea of Marmara
Izmit
Dardanelles
Gallipoli
Adapazari
Sakarya
Bursa
Balikesir
Eskişehir
Kütahya
Zonguldak
T   U
Manisa
Izmir
Ephesus Pamukkale
L. Eğridir
Kuşadasi
Isparta
Denizli
L. Beyşehir
Antalya

AEGEAN SEA

MEDITERRANEAN

🏭 INDUSTRY
Wheat, corn, sugar beets, nuts, fruit, cotton, tobacco, tourism. Carpet-weaving is a centuries-old tradition. Figs and peaches are grown on the coast of the Mediterranean.

🧪 ENVIRONMENT
Turkey's dam-building projects on the Tigris and Euphrates Rivers have met with disapproval from Syria and Iraq, whose own rivers will have reduced flow as a result.

👥 PEOPLE
The Kurds are Turkey's main minority group and one of the largest groups of stateless people in the world. Their homeland, Kurdistan, straddles three countries: Turkey, Iraq, and Iran. Kurds are fighting for the recognition of their rights within Turkey.

E   F   G   H

NATURAL FEATURES
Turkey lies within the Alpine-Himalayan mountain belt. The Arabian, African, Eurasian, Aegean, and Turkish plates all converge within its borders, resulting in severe seismic activity.

CLIMATE
Coastal regions of Turkey and Cyprus have a Mediterranean climate. The Turkish interior has cold, snowy winters and hot, dry summers.

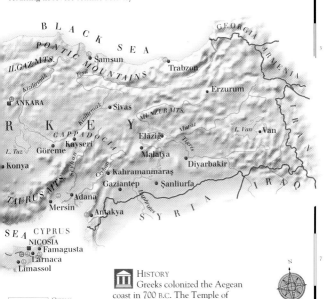

BLACK SEA

PONTIC MOUNTAINS

ILGAZ MTS.

Kızılırmak

Yeşil

•Samsun

Trabzon

GEORGIA

ARMENIA

◆ANKARA

Kızılırmak

•Sivas

•Erzurum

MUNZUR MTS.

Murat

Tigris

L. Van •Van

IRAN

R   K   E   Y

CAPPADOCIA

•Kayseri

•Elazığ

•Malatya

•Diyarbakir

L. Tuz   •Göreme

•Konya

TAURUS MTS.

Seyhan

Ceyhan

•Kahramanmaraş

•Gaziantep   •Şanlıurfa

Euphrates

S Y R I A

IRAQ

•Adana

•Mersin

•Antakya

SEA   CYPRUS

■NICOSIA

•Famagusta

◆Larnaca

•Limassol

CYPRUS
P 708,000
L Greek (Turkish)

HISTORY
Greeks colonized the Aegean coast in 700 B.C. The Temple of Artemis in the city of Ephesus is one of the seven wonders of the ancient world.

N

0   150   300km
0   100   150miles

THE NEAR EAST

AT THE JUNCTION of Africa, Asia, and Europe, the Near East is a mosaic of deserts, mountains, and fertile valleys. After centuries of conflict, there are now hopes for peace in the region. Lebanon is beginning to emerge from a civil war that began in 1975 and the disputes over territories in Israel, such as the West Bank and the Gaza Strip, are starting to be resolved.

LEBANON
P 2.8 million
L Arabic

INDUSTRY
Oil, potash, cotton, fruit. Water is in short supply in this region and special irrigation techniques are used in order to avoid waste. Syria's main cash crop is cotton.

ISRAEL
P 5.3 million
L Hebrew, Arabic

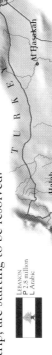

Syria
P 13.4 million
L Arabic

CLIMATE

On the Mediterranean coast, the climate is mild, with wet winters and hot, dry summers. Inland, countries in this region are mostly arid. In the mountains, snow is common in winter.

NATURAL FEATURES

Lying in the valley that forms a part of the Great Rift Valley, the Dead Sea is 399 m (1,310 ft) below sea level. No fish live in its water, which has salt levels six times higher than in other seas.

HISTORY

The history of three major religions – Judaism, Islam, and Christianity – is bound up in the city of Jerusalem. The city contains holy sites such as the Wailing Wall, the Dome of the Rock, and the Church of the Holy Sepulchre.

Jordan
P 4.1 million
L Arabic

N

100km

0   25   50

0   50miles

SYRIAN DESERT

ARABIA

SAUDI ARABIA

Haifa
Caesarea
Tiberias
ISRAEL
Irbid
WEST BANK
Tel Aviv-Yafo
Holon
'Az Zarqā'
AMMAN
JERUSALEM
JORDAN
Gaza
GAZA STRIP
En Gedi
Dead Sea
Beersheba
Petra
NEGEV DESERT
Elat
Al 'Aqabah
EGYPT
Gulf of 'Aqaba
SINAI
300
Gulf of Suez

THE MIDDLE EAST

ISLAM WAS FOUNDED in A.D. 570 in Mecca, Saudi Arabia, and spread throughout the Middle East, where today it is the main religion. Oil has brought wealth to the region but in 1991, the area was devastated by the Gulf War.

INDUSTRY
Oil, natural gas, fishing, carpet-weaving, offshore banking. Saudi Arabia has the world's largest oil reserves. Over 60 per cent of the world's desalination plants are used in this region to make sea water drinkable.

CLIMATE
Most of the countries in this region are semi-arid, with low rainfall. Inland, summer temperatures can reach 48°C (119°F) with winter temperatures falling to freezing.

HISTORY
Ancient civilizations developed about 5,500 years ago in Mesopotamia, between the Tigris and Euphrates Rivers. The Sumerian civilization had advanced methods of irrigation, sophisticated architecture, and a form of writing called cuneiform.

IRAQ
P 20.7 million
L Arabic

SAUDI ARABIA
P 17.5 million
L Arabic

KUWAIT
P 2.1 million
L Arabic

BAHRAIN
P 570,000
L Arabic

QATAR
P 500,000
L Arabic

UNITED ARAB EMIRATES
P 2.6 million
L Arabic

YEMEN
P 12.5 million
L Arabic

EGYPT

JORDAN

AN

HEJAZ

Gulf of Aqaba

RED

Mecca

Jedda

SEA

Abha

Hodeida

Al Mukhā

Bab el Mande

IRAN
P 61.6 million
L Farsi

OMAN
P 1.6 million
L Arabic

Map labels:

E · G · H

TURKEY
AZERBAIJAN
L. Urmia
CASPIAN SEA
TURKMENISTAN
Mosul
Ardabīl
Irbil
Rasht
Kirkūk
Zanjān
As Sulaymāniyah
Sanandaj
ELBURZ MTS.
Sari
SYRIA
I R A Q
TEHRĀN
Semnān
Mashhad
BAGHDĀD
Bākhtarān
Qom
Karbalā
Īlām
Arāk
DASHT-E KAVIR
AFGHANISTAN
Al-Hillah
An-Najaf
Dezfūl
Eşfahān
Al-Amārah
RIAN
SERT
NAFUD
An Nāşirīyah
Aḥvāz
Yazd
Al-Basrah
Ābādān
Yāsūj
Z A G R O S M T S.
KUWAIT CITY
Kermān
DASHT-E LŪT
PAKISTAN
KUWAIT
Shīrāz
Persian
Gulf
Zāhedān
Buraydah
Ad
Bandar-e Abbās
Jaz Mūriān
Dammām
Salt Lake
NEJD
MANAMA
BAHRAIN
RIYADH
Al Hufūf
DOHA
Strait of
Khasab
AD DAHNA
QATAR
Hormuz
(to Oman)
ABU DHABI
Dubai
S A U D I
UNITED ARAB
EMIRATES
Gulf of Oman
A R A B I A
MUSCAT
O M A N
RUB' AL KHALI
RAMLAT AS SAB'ATAYN
Masīrah I.
SAN'A
Gulf of Masīrah
Y E M E N
HADHRAMAUT
Aden
A R A B I A N   S E A

N

0   300   600km
0   150   300miles

E · F · G · H

CENTRAL ASIA

FOR CENTURIES, many people in central Asia lived in mountains as nomads, or in cities that sprung up along the Silk Road. When the region came under Soviet rule, industry was developed and irrigation schemes made farming possible.

INDUSTRY
Cotton, gold, gas, sulphur, mercury, opium, hydroelectricity. Uzbekistan has the largest single gold mine in the world. Tajikistan has 14 per cent of the world's known uranium resources.

HISTORY
In the early 1900s, most of this region, except for Afghanistan, came under Soviet rule, which restricted the use of local languages and Islam. Today, these newly independent countries are resuming the religions, languages, and traditions of their past.

TURKMENISTAN
P 3.9 million
L Turkmen, Russian

ENVIRONMENT
Crop irrigation draws water from the Amu Darya river, reducing the amount of water flowing into the Aral Sea. By the year 2000, the Sea will have shrunk to an estimated third of its original size.

USTYURT PLATEAU

ARAL SEA

TURAN LOWLAND

L. Sarykamysh

Nukus

UZBE

CASPIAN SEA

Zaliv Kara-Bogaz-Gol

Tashauz

Urgench

Krasnovodsk

Nebit Dag

TURKMENISTAN

⊕ ASHKABAD

I R A N

Karakum

Murgab

Tedzhen

Herāt

A F G

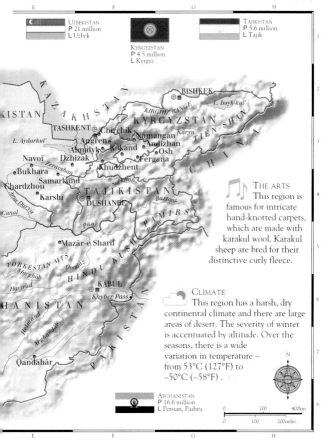

UZBEKISTAN
P 21 million
L Uzbek

KYRGYZSTAN
P 4.5 million
L Kyrgyz

TAJIKISTAN
P 5.6 million
L Tajik

KAZAKHSTAN

BISHKEK

KIRGHIZ RANGE

L. Issyk-kul'

TASHKENT · Chirchik
L. Aydarkul'   KYRGYZSTAN
Angren · Namangan
Almalyk· Kokand ·Andizhan   TIEN SHAN
Navoi Dzhizak   ·Osh
       Zeravshan   Fergana   CHINA
·Bukhara   Khudzhent
Chardzhou Samarkand
Amu Darya · Karshi   TAJIKISTAN
Canal   ⊕ DUSHANBE   Surkhob
                        Bartang
                    P A M I R S
·Mazār-e Sharif   Panj
                   Panj
TURKESTAN MTS.   Qonduz
Morghāb   HINDU KUSH
Harīrūd   ⊕ KABUL
·ANISTAN   Khyber Pass
Helmand   PAKISTAN
    Arghandāb
·Qandahār

THE ARTS
This region is famous for intricate hand-knotted carpets, which are made with karakul wool. Karakul sheep are bred for their distinctive curly fleece.

CLIMATE
This region has a harsh, dry continental climate and there are large areas of desert. The severity of winter is accentuated by altitude. Over the seasons, there is a wide variation in temperature – from 53°C (127°F) to –50°C (–58°F).

AFGHANISTAN
P 16.6 million
L Persian, Pashtu

N

0   200   400km
0   100   200miles

THE RUSSIAN FEDERATION AND KAZAKHSTAN

THE URAL mountains separate European and Asian Russia, which extends from the frozen arctic lands in the north to the central Asian deserts in the south. In 1991, Kazakhstan became the last Soviet republic to gain independence.

CLIMATE
Kazakhstan has a continental climate. Winter temperatures in Russia vary little from north to south, but fall sharply in the east, especially in Siberia.

PEOPLE
There are 57 nationalities with their own territories within the Russian Federation. A further 95 groups have no territories of their own, although these groups make up only six per cent of the population.

KAZAKHSTAN
P 17 million
L Kazakh

Murmansk
BARENTS SEA
FINLAND
ESTONIA
LATVIA
St. Petersburg
Pskov • Novgorod
Arkhangel'sk
BELORUSSIA
Smolensk
MOSCOW
Yaroslavl'
UKRAINE
Tula
Voronezh
Ryazan'
Kirov
Penza
Kazan'
Izhevsk
Perm'
Rostov-na-Donu
Simbirsk
Naberezhnyye Chelny
Saratov
Samara
Yekaterinburg
Krasnodar
Tol'yatti
Ufa
Chelyabinsk
Volgograd
Ural'sk
Orenburg
Omsk
GEORGIA
Astrakhan
Ural
Aktyubinsk
Kustanaj
Groznyy
Atyrau
Emba
Tselinograd
CASPIAN SEA
KIRGHIZ STEPPE
L. Tengiz
UZBEKISTAN
ARAL SEA
Karaganda
KAZAKHSTAN
Syr Darya
Kzyl-Orda
L. Balkhash
Chu
TURKMENISTAN
UZBEKISTAN
Shymkent
ALMA-ATA
URAL MOUNTAINS
Irtysh
Ishim

HISTORY

Kazakhstan was absorbed by Russia in the 19th century, when Russians began to settle the land used by nomadic Kazakhs. Settlement and industrial development increased after 1917.

INDUSTRY

Oil, gas, coal, gold, diamonds. Mineral-rich Kazakhstan has the world's largest chromium mine. Siberia has large gas, coal, and oil fields.

Bering St.

Wrangel I.

CHUKCHI SEA

C. Navarin

Anadyr'

Ayon Is.

EAST SIBERIAN SEA

BERING SEA

Cape Olyutorskiy

KORYAK RANGE

Karaginskiy Is.

Bear Is.

New Siberian Is.

ovaya emlya

Severnaya Zemlya

Bolshevik I.

C. Chelyuskin

LAPTEV SEA

Belyy I.

Olenek Bay

Olenek

Indigirka

Kolyma

Korkodon

KOLYMA RANGE

KAMCHATKA

TAYMYR PENINSULA

L. Taymyr

Pyasina

Khatanga

VERKHOYANSK RANGE

Yana

Magadan

Petropavlovsk- Kamchatskiy

GYDA PENINSULA

CENTRAL SIBERIAN PLATEAU

Kotuy

Aldan

Lena

C. Lopatka

Paramushir Is.

ENINSULA

Nakhodka

BERIAN

Noril'sk

PUTORANA MTS.

RUSSIAN

Viluy

Aldma

Yakutsk

SEA OF OKHOTSK

C. Yelizavety

Vakh

Taz

Ob'

Yenisey

Lower Tunguska

FEDERATION

Amga

Aldan

DZHUGDZHUR RANGE

Ket'

SIBERIA

Stony Tunguska

Lena

Vitim

Olëkma

Sakhalin

Angara

Zeya Res.

Tomsk

Krasnoyarsk

L. Baikal

STANOVOY RANGE

Shilka

Blagoveshchensk

Khabarovsk

Novosibirsk

Novokuznetsk

Abakan

Angarsk

Ulan-Ude

Amur

arnaul

Biysk

Kyzyl

Irkutsk

CHINA

Vladivostok

empatinsk

MONGOLIA

SEA OF JAPAN

Yuzhno- Sakhalinsk

Kurile Islands

NORTH KOREA

Lavson

RUSSIAN FEDERATION
P 148.7 million
L Russian

| 0 | 600 | 1200km |
| 0 | 300 | 600miles |

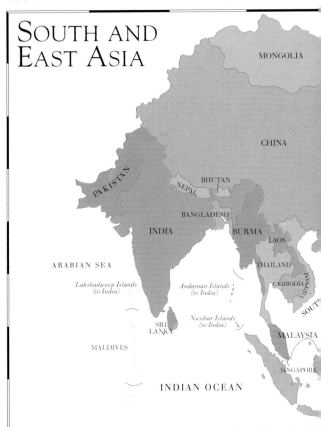

SOUTH AND EAST ASIA

MONGOLIA

CHINA

PAKISTAN

NEPAL

BHUTAN

BANGLADESH

INDIA

BURMA

LAOS

THAILAND

CAMBODIA

VIETNAM

SOUT

ARABIAN SEA

Lakshadweep Islands
(to India)

Andaman Islands
(to India)

SRI
LANKA

Nicobar Islands
(to India)

MALAYSIA

MALDIVES

SINGAPORE

INDIAN OCEAN

NORTH KOREA

SOUTH KOREA

SEA OF JAPAN

JAPAN

TAIWAN

Hong Kong
(to U.K.)

Macao
Portugal)

NA SEA

PHILIPPINES

UNEI

NDONESIA

SOUTH AND EAST ASIA

From the dry deserts of Mongolia to the tropical rainforests of Malaysia, the Philippines, and Indonesia, Asia is a continent of great contrasts. It is a mountainous region and contains the world's highest mountain, Mount Everest.

PACIFIC OCEAN

Northern Mariana Islands
(to U.S.A.)

Guam
(to U.S.A.)

MARSHALL ISLANDS

MICRONESIA

PALAU

THE INDIAN SUBCONTINENT

SEPARATED FROM THE rest of Asia by the Himalayas, India is the second most populated country after China. It is estimated that India's population will overtake that of China by 2030. To the north, Nepal and Bhutan lie nestled in the Himalayas between China and India. To the south lies Sri Lanka, once known as Ceylon.

INDUSTRY
Tea, jute, iron, cut diamonds, cotton, rice, sugar cane, textiles. Bangladesh exports 80 per cent of the world's jute fibre. Sri Lanka is the largest tea exporter in the world. Pakistan is a major exporter of rice.

HISTORY
In 1947, when India gained independence, religious differences led to the creation of two countries – Hindu India and Muslim Pakistan. In 1971, a short civil war broke out between East and West Pakistan and East Pakistan became Bangladesh.

INDIA
P 879.5 million
L Hindi, English

NATURAL FEATURES
The Himalayas were formed as a result of a violent crumpling of the Earth's crust. Frequent earthquakes indicate that the process is continuing. The highest peaks in the world, including Mount Everest, are in this mountain system.

AFGHANISTAN
CHAGAI HILLS
IRAN
PAKISTAN
MAKRAN
Indus
THA
Hyderabad
Karachi
ARABIAN SEA
Gulf of Kutch
Rajkot
Gulf of Khambha

N

0   350   700km
0   200   400miles

PESHAWAR
ISLAMABAD
Rawalpindi
Gujranwala
Lahore Amritsar
Faisalabad Jalandhar
Multan Ludhiana Chandigarh
DESERT
NEW Meerut
DELHI Bareilly
Jaipur Agra
Gwalior
Jodhpur Kota
Gandi Res.
Ahmadabad Kanpur Varanasi
Allahabad Patna
Bhopal Jabalpur
Indore Narmada
Vadodara
Surat Tapti Nagpur
Nasik
Thane
Bombay DECCAN Godavari
Pune
Sholapur
Krishna
Hyderabad
Panaji PLATEAU
Dharwad
EASTERN GHATS
Mangalore
Bangalore Madras
Coimbatore
MALABAR COAST
Cochin
Madurai Jaffna
Trivandrum
SRI LANKA
COLOMBO
Galle

HIMALAYA
CHINA
Srinagar
Ganges
KATHMANDU THIMBU
Lucknow BHUTAN
Brahmaputra
Rajshahi BANGLADESH
Guwahati
Imphal
Dhanbad DACCA Agartala
Ranchi Calcutta Khulna
Chittagong
Mahanadi
Vishakhapatnam
Vijayawada
CORONDEL COAST
Bay of Bengal
BURMA

PAKISTAN
P 122.4 million
L Urdu

BHUTAN
P 1.6 million
L Dzongkha

NEPAL
P 20.4 million
L Nepali

BANGLADESH
P 119.3 million
L Bengali

SRI LANKA
P 17.7 million
L Sinhalese,
Tamil

CLIMATE

Sri Lanka and southern
India are tropical, with little
seasonal variation in temperature.
The north has a cold alpine climate.
Cyclones regularly build up in the
Bay of Bengal, and Bangladesh is
often flooded during the monsoon.

CHINA AND MONGOLIA

ISOLATED FROM THE western world for centuries, the Chinese were the first to develop the compass, paper, gunpowder, porcelain, and silk. Three autonomous regions lie within western China – Inner Mongolia, Xinjiang, and Tibet. The Gobi desert in vast Mongolia is the world's most northern desert.

PEOPLE
Han Chinese make up 93 per cent of China's population. China has relaxed its 1979 one-child policy for minority groups, such as the Mongolians, Tibetans, and Muslim Uygurs, after some groups faced near extinction.

HISTORY
Tibet was invaded by China in 1950. The Chinese destroyed Tibet's traditional agricultural society and brutally repressed Buddhism. In 1959 there were more than 6,000 Buddhist monasteries – by 1980, only 179 remained.

KAZAKHSTAN

L. Aya

Hari L. Sk.

ALTAI MTS.

XINJIANG UIGHUR

Ürümqi

AUTONOMOUS

TIEN MTS.

Tarim

L. Bosten

REGION

Tarim Basin

Lop Nur

KYRGYZSTAN

TAKLA MAKAN DESERT

TAJIKISTAN

AFGHANISTAN

PAKISTAN

KARAKORAM

Aksai Chin (Controlled by China, claimed by India)

ALTUN MTS.

KUNLUN MTS.

TIBETAN

BAYAN

Demchok (Claimed by both China and India)

AUTONOMOUS

TANGGULA MTS.

REGION

GANGDISE RANGE

Brahmaputra (Yarlung Zangbo)

Lhasa

HIMALAYAS

NEPAL

BHUTAN

INDIA

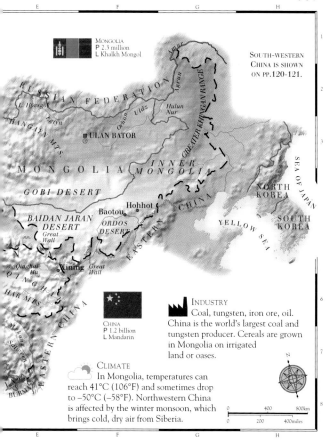

MONGOLIA
P 2.3 million
L Khalkh Mongol

SOUTH-WESTERN
CHINA IS SHOWN
ON PP.120-121.

RUSSIAN FEDERATION

L. Hövsgöl

HANGAYN MTS.

Tegiyn

Onon

Uldz

Hulun
Nur

⊕ ULAN BATOR

GREATER KHINGAN RANGE

M O N G O L I A

INNER
MONGOLIA

NORTH
KOREA

SEA OF JAPAN

GOBI DESERT

BAIDAN JARAN
DESERT

Baotou

Hohhot

CHINA

Great
Wall

ORDOS
DESERT

EASTERN

YELLOW
SEA

SOUTH
KOREA

Qinghai
Hu

Xining

Great
Wall

QINGHAI

HAR MTS.

EASTERN CHINA

M.Koo & Schweu

BURMA

CHINA
P 1.2 billion
L Mandarin

INDUSTRY
Coal, tungsten, iron ore, oil.
China is the world's largest coal and
tungsten producer. Cereals are grown
in Mongolia on irrigated
land or oases.

CLIMATE
In Mongolia, temperatures can
reach 41°C (106°F) and sometimes drop
to –50°C (–58°F). Northwestern China
is affected by the winter monsoon, which
brings cold, dry air from Siberia.

N

0   400   800km

0   200   400miles

CHINA AND KOREA

ONE-FIFTH of the world's population live in China – mostly in the eastern part of the country. Annexed to Japan in 1910, Korea was divided between the U.S.A. and Communist Russia after World War II. North and South Korea were formed in 1948.

NORTH-WESTERN CHINA IS SHOWN ON PP. 118–119.

RUSSIAN FEDERATION

LESSER KHINGAN MTS.

Amur

Qiqihar

Harbin

MANCHURIA

Changchun

Jilin

Shenyang

Fushun

Anshan

Dalian

Bo Hai

Tangshan

Tientsin

YELLOW SEA

Shandong Pen.

Qingdao

Zibo

Jinan

Handan

Zhengzhou

Zaozhuang

Luoyang

Xi'an

QIN LING

Chengdu

Chungking

WESTERN CHINA

LOESS HILLS
AUTONOMOUS
REGION

Lanzhou

Great Wall

Great Wall

Yellow River

Taiyuan

Shijiazhuang

PEKING

Datong

Tabong

Yinsha

Yangtze

MONGOLIA

CHINA

Huainan

Hefei

Nanjing

Wuxi

Wuhan

Shanghai

Hangzhou

Shaoxing

Ningbo

Chŏngjin

NORTH KOREA

Sinŭiju

PYONGYANG

Namp'o

Incheon

SEOUL

SOUTH KOREA

Taejŏn

Taegu

Pusan

Cheju

Korea Strait

EAST CHINA SEA

NORTH KOREA
P 22.6 million
L Korean

SOUTH KOREA
P 44.2 million
L Korean

TAIWAN
P 20.8 million
L Mandarin

CHINA
P 1.2 billion
L Mandarin

EAST

TAIPEI
TAIWAN
Kao-hsiung

Fuzhou
Xiamen

Nanchang
Changsha

Dongting Hu
Yuan

Guiyang

Kunming

Wujiang He

Guangxi Zhuang
AUTONOMOUS
REGION
Nanning

Canton Dongguan
Kowloon
HONG KONG
(to U.K.)
MACAO
(to Portugal)
Leizhou Pen.
Gulf of
Tongking
Haikou

Hainan

SOUTH CHINA SEA

Taiwan Strait

VIETNAM
LAOS
BURMA

Mekong
Salween

PEOPLE

Korea has been inhabited by one ethnic group for 2,000 years and even today those with the same surname group may not marry each other. Most Taiwanese are descendants of the Chinese supporters of the deposed Ming dynasty, who migrated in 1644.

CLIMATE

Southern South Korea and Taiwan have a tropical monsoon climate similar to that of southern China. North Korea has a continental climate.

HISTORY

In 1949, the People's Republic of China was established as a communist state, and Taiwan became a separate country.

COMMUNICATIONS

South Korea has one of the world's best public transport systems. Buses, trains, boats, and planes are all integrated in one timetable.

INDUSTRY

Rice, electronics, wheat, finance, textiles. Hong Kong has the busiest container port in the world. Taiwan is the world's leading producer of watches, computers, televisions, and track shoes.

100   300   600km
0
150   300miles

N

JAPAN

CONSISTING OF FOUR main islands and 4,000 smaller ones, Japan is the world's leading industrial nation. Since two-thirds of the land is mountainous, the majority of people live on the coast. Japan has about 1,500 minor earthquakes a year, but severe earthquakes, such as the one in Kobe in 1994, occur every few years. Underwater earthquakes sometimes cause huge surge waves, or *tsunami*, along Japan's Pacific coast.

Habomai Is.

Kuril Islands

Yekaterina Strait

La Pérouse Strait   SEA OF OKHOTSK

Hokkaidō

ISHIKARI MTS.

HIDAKA MTS.

Ishikari Bay

Sapporo

Uchiura Bay

Tsugaru Strait

OU MTS.

Mogami

Sendai

Shinano

Toyama Bay

SEA OF JAPAN

INDUSTRY
Fishing, ship building, motor vehicles, computers, televisions, high-tech electronics. Motor vehicles are Japan's biggest export, and its stock exchange ranks second in the world. Japan excels at producing miniature electronic goods.

HISTORY
Japan was once ruled by warlords called *shoguns*, who discouraged contact with the outside world. In 1639, Japan cut ties with other nations and ordered all Europeans to leave, except the Dutch who were allowed one trading ship per year.

JAPAN
P 124.5 million
L Japanese

NATURAL FEATURES

Situated on an unstable part of the Earth's crust, Japan is prone to earthquakes and volcanic activity. There are more than 150 major volcanoes in Japan (over 60 of which are active). These form part of the "Ring of Fire" that runs along the edge of the Pacific Ocean.

CLIMATE

The Sea of Japan has a moderating influence on Japan's climate. Winters are not as cold as on the Asian mainland, and Japan has a much higher rainfall – most of which falls in summer.

COMMUNICATIONS

The *Shinkansen*, or bullet train, is the second fastest in the world. With an average speed of 195 km/h (122 mph) it is renowned for both its speed and reliability.

PEOPLE

The Japanese, both young and old, are avid readers of comic books, known as *manga* and newspapers. Also popular are lifestyle magazines, which encourage the Japanese to make more use of their limited leisure time.

Map labels:

PACIFIC OCEAN

Kasumi Lagoon
Chiba
TOKYO
Kawasaki   Yokohama
Nagoya
Sagami Sea
Sea of Japan
Kyoto
Kobe   Osaka
L. Biwa
Wakasa Bay
Hamada
Okayama
Hiroshima
Oki Is.
Shikoku
Kumamoto
Kitakyūshū
Fukuoka
Kyūshū
Kagoshima
Ōsumi Strait
Ōsumi Is.
Tokara Is.
Korea Strait
Gotō Is.
Amami Is.
AMAKUSA SEA
EAST CHINA SEA
Ryūkyū Is.
Okinawa Is.
Okinawa

N

0   150   300km
0   75   150miles

MAINLAND SOUTHEAST ASIA

FOR MOST of its history, Thailand has been an independent kingdom. Malaysia includes 11 states on the mainland (Malaya), as well as Sabah and Sarawak in Borneo. Cambodia, Laos, and Vietnam have suffered from years of civil war. Burma has become more and more isolated from the world by its repressive government.

BURMA (MYANMAR)
P 43.7 million
L Burmese
(Myanmar)

Laos
P 4.6 million
L Lao

Map labels

INDIA

CHINA

BURMA

BANG DESH

Bay of Bengal

CHIN Hills

Chindwin

Irrawaddy

Monywa
Sagaing · Amarapura
Mandalay
Pakokku
Taunggyi
L. Inle
Minbu
Pyinmana
Prome
Sandoway
Henzada

Salween

Sittang

Mekong

L. Thac Ba
Red R.
Black R.
Nam Ou
Viet Tri
Thac Ba
Thai Nguyen
Hong Gai
HANOI
Nam Dinh
Thanh
Hoa
Vinh

Nam Ma
Louang
Phrabang
Nam Than

LAOS

Chiang Mai

VIETNAM

HONG KONG

Gulf of Tongking

Bai Phong

Gulf of

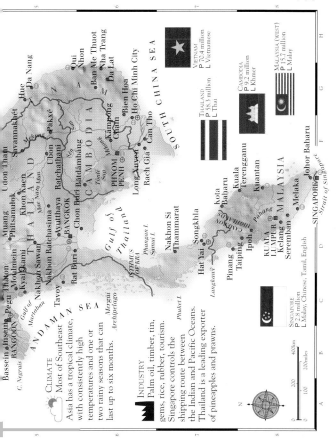

Bassein • Insein • Pegu • Thaton
RANGOON • Moulmein
C. Negrais • Kyaikkami
Mae Nam Yom

Muang • Udon Thani
Phitsanulok
Nakhon Sawan
Khon Kaen
Mae Nam Mun

Savannakhét
Pakxé

VIETNAM
P 72.4 million
L Vietnamese

THAILAND
Kyaikkami • Tavoy
T H A I L A N D
BANGKOK
Nakhon Ratchasima
Ayuthaya
Rat Buri
Chon Buri Batdâmbâng

C A M B O D I A
PHNOM
PENH
Long Xuyen
Rach Gia • Can Tho

Hue
Da Nang
Qui
Nhon
Ban Me Thuot • Nha Trang
Da Lat
Bien Hoa
Kâmpóng
Cham
Ho Chi Minh City

CAMBODIA
P 9.2 million
L Khmer

MALAYSIA (WEST)
P 15.7 million
L Malay

THAILAND
P 58.3 million
L Thai

S O U T H   C H I N A   S E A

A N D A M A N   S E A

Gulf of
Thailand

Phangan I.
Samui I.

ISTHMUS
OF KRA

Nakhon Si
Thammarat
Songkhla

Langkawi
Phuket I.
Hat Yai

Kota
Baharu
Kuala
Terengganu
Kuantan

Pinang
Taiping • Ipoh
KUALA
LUMPUR • Kelang
Seremban

M A L A Y S I A
Pahang
Meleka

SINGAPORE
Strait of Singapore

Johor Baharu

SINGAPORE
P 2.8 million
L Malay, Chinese, Tamil, English

CLIMATE
Most of Southeast Asia has a tropical climate, with consistently high temperatures and one or two rainy seasons that can last up to six months.

INDUSTRY
Palm oil, timber, tin, gems, rice, rubber, tourism. Singapore controls the shipping route between the Indian and Pacific Oceans. Thailand is a leading exporter of pineapples and prawns.

N

0   200   400km
0   100   200miles

MARITIME SOUTHEAST ASIA

SCATTERED BETWEEN the Indian and Pacific Oceans are thousands of tropical mountainous islands. Once called the East Indies, Indonesia was ruled by the Dutch for 350 years. More than half of its 13,677 islands are still uninhabited. The Philippines lie on the "Ring of Fire", and are subject to earthquakes and volcanic activity. Borneo is shared among Indonesia, Malaysia, and Brunei.

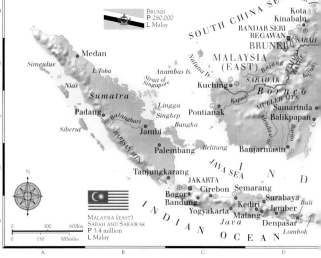

PHILI

Balabac Strait

SOUTH CHINA SEA

BRUNEI
P 280,000
L Malay

Kota Kinabalu

BANDAR SERI BEGAWAN

SABAH

BRUNEI

MALAYSIA (EAST)

CRUMPET RANGE

Medan

L. Toba

Anambas Is.

Natuna Is.

Rajang

Simeulue

Nias

Sumatra

Strait of Singapore

SARAWAK

Kuching

Borneo

MULLER MTS.

Samarinda

Kapuas

Kayan

Lingga

Pontianak

Padang

Batanghari

Singkep

Bangka

Balikpapan

Siberut

Jambi

BARISAN MTS.

Palembang

Belitung

Banjarmasin

Mendawai

JAVA SEA

Tanjungkarang

I

N

JAKARTA

Bogor

Cirebon

Semarang

Bandung

Kediri

Surabaya

Yogyakarta

Malang

Jember

Bali

Java

Denpasar

Lombok

D

N

I

N

D

I

A

N

O

C

E

A

N

MALAYSIA (EAST)
SABAH AND SARAWAK
P 3.4 million
L Malay

0   300   600km
0   150   300miles

F G H

Luzon Strait

Luzon

Baguio
Dagupan
ngeles Cabanatuan
MANILA
Lucena

PHILIPPINES
P 65.6 million
L Filipino, English

Batangas
Mindoro Legaspi
Mindoro Naga
Strait
Panay Cadiz
Palawan Iloilo Samar
Bacolod Tacloban
PPINES Negros Cebu
Butuan
Cagayan de Oro
Iligan Mindanao
Zamboanga Davao
Jolo
Sulu Archipelago General
Santos
Talaud Is.

PHILIPPINE SEA

SULU SEA

CELEBES SEA

Makassar Strait

Manado
Gulf of
Tomini
Palu Sula Is.
Celebes

Kendari Buru Ambon
Seram

Ujung Pandang

FLORES SEA
Sumbawa
Lesser Sunda Islands
Flores Timor
Kupang
Sumba Roti

MOLUCCA SEA
Halmahera

Moluccas
SERAM SEA

BANDA SEA

TIMOR SEA

PACIFIC OCEAN

Supiori
Biak
Jayapura

IRIAN JAYA
MAOKE MTS.

ARAFURA SEA
Kai Is.
Aru Is.
Dolak

Tanimbar Is.

PAPUA NEW GUINEA

INDONESIA
P 187.8 million
L Bahasa Indonesia

INDUSTRY
Palm oil, timber, rice, oil, natural gas, copper, chrome, tourism. Malaysia is the largest producer of palm oil and computer disk-drives. Indonesia is a major exporter of natural gas.

ENVIRONMENT
Logging, especially in Borneo and the Philippines, is a problem in the region. Forest communities, like the Malaysian Penan, are being destroyed. Some tree species are near extinction.

CLIMATE
Countries situated around the equator are hot and humid all year. Variations in climate are related to latitude.

F G H

PACIFIC OCEAN

THE LARGEST AND deepest
ocean, the Pacific covers a
greater area of the Earth's surface
than all the land areas together.
Its deepest point – 11,033 m
(36,197ft) – is deep enough
to cover Mount Everest.
Melanesia, Micronesia,
and Polynesia are the
main inner Pacific
island groups.

MICRONESIA
P 104,000
L English

NAURU
P 9,400
L Nauruan, English

NATURAL FEATURES

Some Pacific islands are
coral atolls – ring-shaped islands
or chains of islands surrounding
a lagoon. They are formed when
coral builds up on a sunken bank or
on a volcano crater in the open sea.

SOLOMON
ISLANDS
P 349,500
L English

ENVIRONMENT

Nuclear testing by
the U.S.A. and France has
dangerously polluted areas in
the South Pacific. Countries
such as Japan, Australia, and
New Zealand want the region
made into a nuclear-free zone.

VANUATU
P 163,000
L Bislama,
English, French

FIJI
P 758,300
L English

N

| 0 | 1500 | 3000km |
| 0 | 750 | 1500miles |

SEA OF
OKHOTSK

ASIA

SEA OF JAPAN

Yokohama
Kōbe

Shanghai

Hong Kong

Manila

GUAM
(to U.S.A.)

NORTHERN
MARIANAS IS.

MARSHALL
ISLANDS

MICRONESIA

FEDERATED STATES
OF MICRONESIA

NAURU

SOUTH
EAST ASIA

ARAFURA
SEA

CORAL
SEA

Great
Barrier
Reef

AUSTRALIA

NEW
CALEDONIA
(to France)

Sydney

TASMAN
SEA

ARCTI

P

SOUT

OCEAN

NORTH AMERICA

Bering Strait
BERING SEA
Aleutian Trench
Aleutian Is.
Gulf of Alaska
Yukon
Vancouver
Seattle

CIFIC
CEAN

Mendocino Fracture Zone
San Francisco
Long Beach
MIDWAY IS.
(to U.S.A.)
Murray Fracture Zone

Pacific Seamounts
HONOLULU
Hawaii

Clarion Fracture Zone

CENTRAL AMERICA

Clipperton Fracture Zone

Albatross Plateau
Panama City

KIRIBATI

Galápagos Is.
(to Ecuador)

TOKELAU
(to N.Z.)
AMERICAN SAMOA
(to U.S.A.)

Marquesas Is.

SOUTH AMERICA

WALLIS & FUTUNA
COOK ISLANDS
(to N.Z.)
NIUE
(to N.Z.)
Tahiti
Tuamotu Archipelago

Callao

East Pacific Rise

TONGA
FRENCH POLYNESIA
PITCAIRN IS.
(to U.K.)

WESTERN SAMOA

NEW ZEALAND

Southwest Pacific Basin

Valparaíso

Wellington

Pacific Antarctic Ridge

C. Horn

HERN OCEAN

Pacific
South East Pacific Basin

ANTARCTICA

MARSHALL ISLANDS
P 52,000
L English, Marshallese

KIRIBATI
P 77,000
L English, Gilbertese

TONGA
P 105,000
L Tongan, English

WESTERN SAMOA
P 169,000
L Samoan, English

TUVALU
P 10,000
L Tuvaluan, English

AUSTRALASIA

NAURU

PAPUA NEW GUINEA

SOLOMON ISLANDS

TU

Coral Sea Islands (to Australia)

VANUATU

New Caledonia (to France)

AUSTRALIA

TASMAN SEA

NEW ZEALAND

SOUTHERN OCEAN

Auckland Islands (to N.Z.)

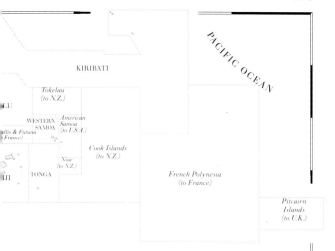

KIRIBATI

Tokelau
(to N.Z.)

WESTERN   American
SAMOA   Samoa
           (to U.S.A.)
allis & Futuna
France)

LU

Cook Islands
(to N.Z.)

Niue
(to N.Z.)

TONGA

French Polynesia
(to France)

IJI

Pitcairn
Islands
(to U.K.)

Chatham Island
(to N.Z.)

PACIFIC OCEAN

AUSTRALASIA

Millions of years ago, the continent of
Australia and the islands of New Guinea
and New Zealand split away from the
other southern continents. These island
countries have many unique plants and
animals, such as Australia's marsupials,
or pouched mammals. The thousands of
islands scattered in the Pacific are either
volcanic islands or coral atolls.

AUSTRALIA AND PAPUA NEW GUINEA

THE SMALLEST, flattest, and driest continent, Australia has a landscape that varies from tropical rainforest to arid desert. Lying to the north, Papua New Guinea (PNG) is so mountainous that its tribes are isolated from each other and from the outside world.

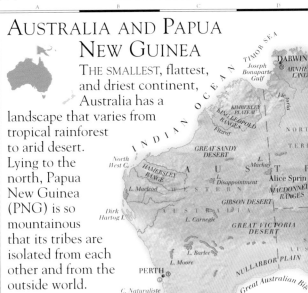

AUSTRALIA
P 17.6 million
L English

CLIMATE

Most people live in temperate zones that occur within 400 km (249 miles) of the coast in the east and southeast, and around Perth in the west. The interior, west, and south are arid; the north is tropical. PNG is tropical, yet snow falls on its highest mountains.

INDUSTRY

Coal, gold, uranium, cattle, tourism, wool, wine- and beer-making. Australia is a leading exporter of coal, iron ore, gold, bauxite, and copper, and has the largest known diamond deposits. PNG has the largest copper mine in the world and one of the largest gold mines.

ARAFURA SEA

Torres Strait

PACIFIC OCEAN

C. Arnhem

CAPE YORK PENINSULA

Gulf of Carpentaria

Mitchell

Great Barrier Reef

ERN

TORY

GREAT DIVIDING RANGE

Townsville

Flinders

SIMPSON DESERT

QUEENSLAND

A L I A

Diamantina

L. Eyre

Cooper Creek

BRISBANE

Gold Coast

FLINDERS RANGES

Darling

NEW SOUTH WALES

Murray

Newcastle

Murrumbidgee

SYDNEY

Wollongong

ADELAIDE

CANBERRA

AUSTRALIAN CAPITAL TERRITORY

Kangaroo I.

VICTORIA

MELBOURNE

Geelong

Bass Strait

Flinders I.

C. Grim

TASMANIA

TASMAN SEA

HOBART

South East C.

N

0   300   600km
0   150   300miles

ARAFURA SEA

Bismarck Archipelago

BISMARCK SEA

New Ireland

New Guinea

INDONESIA

PAPUA NEW GUINEA

New Britain

Fly

SOLOMON SEA

PORT MORESBY

CORAL SEA

PAPUA NEW GUINEA
P 3.9 million
L Pidgin English, Motu, English

PEOPLE
The first people in Australia were Aboriginals, a nomadic people who reached the continent from Southeast Asia about 50,000 years ago.

FLORA AND FAUNA
Due to its isolation, Australia has many unique animals such as koalas and kangaroos. The platypus and the echidna, which is also found in New Guinea, are the only egg-laying mammals.

NATURAL FEATURES
The Great Barrier Reef, a series of coral reefs and islands, stretches over 2,000 km (1,243 miles) just off the coast of Queensland. Composed of coral polyps, it is the largest living organism on Earth.

NEW ZEALAND

ONE OF THE LAST places on Earth to be inhabited by people, New Zealand lies about halfway between the equator and the South Pole. It is made up of the main North and South Islands, separated by the Cook Strait, and numerous smaller islands. The first settlers were Maoris, who came from the Polynesian islands about 1,200 years ago.

NATURAL FEATURES

New Zealand lies on the "Ring of Fire", a band of volcanic activity that almost encircles the Pacific Ocean. New Zealand has about 400 earthquakes each year, although only about 100 are strong enough to be felt.

PEOPLE

In recent years, Maoris have protested the lack of observance of the Treaty of Waitangi, which protected their rights. About 10 per cent of the total population are Maori.

FLORA AND FAUNA

Many of New Zealand's animals have been introduced – two species of bat are the only native land mammals. New Zealand has no snakes.

Great Exhibition Bay

Kaipara Harbour

North Island

Great Barrier I.

Auckland

Hamilton

L. Taupo

Bay of Plenty

Hawke Bay

Napier

TASMAN SEA

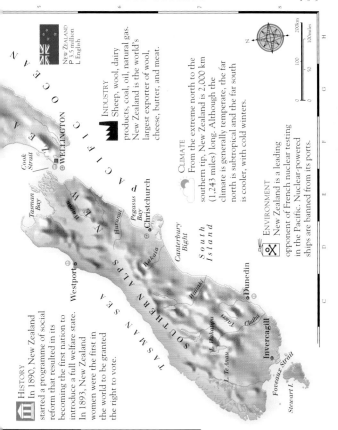

PACIFIC OCEAN

TASMAN SEA

NEW ZEALAND
P 3.5 million
L English

INDUSTRY
Sheep, wool, dairy products, coal, oil, natural gas. New Zealand is the world's largest exporter of wool, cheese, butter, and meat.

CLIMATE
From the extreme north to the southern tip, New Zealand is 2,000 km (1,243 miles) long. Although the climate is generally temperate, the far north is subtropical and the far south is cooler, with cold winters.

ENVIRONMENT
New Zealand is a leading opponent of French nuclear testing in the Pacific. Nuclear-powered ships are banned from its ports.

HISTORY
In 1890, New Zealand started a programme of social reform that resulted in its becoming the first nation to introduce a full welfare state. In 1893, New Zealand women were the first in the world to be granted the right to vote.

N

0   100   200 km
0   50   100 miles

Cook Strait

●WELLINGTON

Tasman Bay

NORTH ISLAND

SOUTHERN ALPS

Westport

Pegasus Bay

Christchurch

Canterbury Bight

South Island

Rakaia

Hurunui

Waitaki

Dunedin

Waitaki

L. Wakatipu

Clutha

L. Te Anau

Invercargill

Foveaux Strait

Stewart I.

Index

Grid references in the Index help find places on the map. If you look up Nairobi in the Index, you will see 96 F4. The first number, 96, is the page number on which the map of Nairobi appears. Next, find the letters and numbers which border the page and trace a line across from the letter and down from the number. This will direct you to the exact grid square in which the city of Nairobi is located.

J

Jabalpur India 117 F4
Jackson USA 28 D4
Jacksonville USA 29 F6
Jaffna Sri Lanka 117 F7
Jaipur India 117 E3
Jakarta Indonesia 126 C7
Jalandhar India 117 E2
Jamaica (Country) 43 E4
Jambi Indonesia 126 B6
James Bay Canada 24 D4
Jan Mayen I. Norway
51 G8
Japan (Country) 122–123
Japan, Sea of E. Asia
113 H6/122 D4/128 D2
Java (I.) Indonesia 101 G5/
126 C8
Java Sea Indonesia 126 C7
Jayapura Indonesia 127 H6
Jedda Saudi Arabia 108 D5
Jefferson City USA 33 H5
Jember Indonesia 126 D8
Jersey (I.) UK 59 F8
Jerusalem Israel 107 C5
Jilin China 120 G2
Jinan China 120 E3
Jingdezhen China 120 F5
Jodhpur India 117 E3
Johannesburg South
Africa 99 E6
Johor Baharu Malaysia
125 E8
Jönköping Sweden 57 C7
Jordan (Country) 107
Juan de Fuca, Strait of
USA/Canada 36 A2
Juneau Alaska 22 D6
Jutland Denmark 57 A7

K

Kabul Afghanistan 111 F6
Kabwe Kenya 97 C7
Kagoshima Japan 123 B6

Kahramanmaraş Turkey
105 F5
Kalahari Desert
Botswana 99 D6
Kalemie Zaire 95 G7
Kaliningrad Rus. Fed.
81 B5
Kamchatka Rus. Fed.
113 H3
Kampala Uganda 96 E3
Kâmpóng Cham
Cambodia 125 F6
Kananga Zaire 95 F7
Kano Nigeria 93 G5
Kanpur India 117 F3
Kansas (State) USA 33 G5
Kansas City USA 33 G5
Kao-hsiung Taiwan
121 F7
Kara Sea Rus. Fed. 51 H5/
82 G3/112 D3
Karachi Pakistan 100 E3/
116 D3
Karaganda Kazakhstan
112 D6
Karakorum Mts. China
118 D3
Karakum Canal
Turkmenistan 110 C4
Karbala Iraq 109 E3
Kariba, Lake Zambia/
Zaire 97 C7/99 E3
Karlsruhe Germany 67 D6
Karpathos (I.) Greece
79 G7
Karshi Uzbekistan 111 E4
Kasai (R.) Zaire 95 E6
Kathmandu Nepal 117 F3
Katowice Poland 71 E5
Kattegat Denmark
57 B7
Kaunas Lithuania 81 C5
Kawasaki Japan 123 F5
Kayseri Turkey 105 E5

Kazakhstan (Country) 112
Kazan' Rus. Fed. 83 D6/
112 C5
Kediri Indonesia 126 D8
Kelang Malaysia 125 D8
Kendari Indonesia 127 E6
Kentucky (State) USA
29 E2
Kenya (Country) 96
Kermān Iran 109 G4
Khabarovsk Rus. Fed.
113 H6
Khadzhent Tajikistan
111 F3
Kharkiv Ukraine 85 E3
Khartoum Sudan 91 D5
Khasab Oman 109 G5
Kherson Ukraine 85 E4
Khmel'nyts'kyy Ukraine
84 D3
Khon Kaen Thailand
125 E5
Khulna Bangladesh
117 G4
Khyber Pass Afghanistan/
Pakistan 111 F6
Kiel Germany 66 E2
Kiev Ukraine 84 D3
Kigali Rwanda 96 D4
Kikwit Zaire 95 E7
Kimberley South Africa
99 D7
King Leopold Range
(Mts.) Australia 132 C3
Kingston Jamaica 43 E4
Kinshasa Zaire 95 D6
Kirghiz Range (Mts.)
Kyrgyzstan 111 G2
Kiribati (Country) 129 E4
Kirkūk Iraq 109 F2
Kirov Rus. Fed. 112 C4
Kisangani Zaire 95 F6
Kismaayo Somalia 91 F8
Kitakyūshū Japan 123 B6

Málaga Spain 61 E7
Malang Indonesia 126 D8
Malatya Turkey 105 F5
Malawi (Country) 97
Malaysia (Country) 125
Malaysia (East) Borneo/
S.E. Asia 126 D5
Maldives (Country) 100 D4
Male Maldives 100 E4
Mali (Country) 95 E4
Malmo Sweden 57 C7
Malta (I.) 73 F8
Mamry, Lake Poland 70 F3
Man, Isle of UK 59 E5
Manado Indonesia 127 F5
Managua Nicaragua 42 B6
Manama Bahrain 109 F5
Manaus Brazil 46 D4
Manchester UK 59 F5
Manchuria China 120 G2
Mandalay Burma 124 C3
Mangalore India 117 E6
Manila Philippines 127 E2
Manisa Turkey 104 C5
Manitoba (Province)
Canada 23 F7
Mannheim Germany
67 D6
Maputo (Mozambique)
99 F6
Mar del Plata Argentina
49 E5
Maracaibo Venezuela
44 C3
Marañón (R.) Peru 45 B5
Maribor Slovenia 74 C3
Mariupol' Ukraine 85 E4
Marmara, Sea of Turkey
104 C3
Maroua Cameroon 94 D4
Marquesas Is. France
129 F5
Marquette USA 31 F3
Marrakesh Morocco 88 D3

Marseilles France 63 F7
Marshall Is. (Country)
128 D4
Martinique France 43 H7
Maryland (State) USA
29 H2
Masai Steppe Tanzania
96 F4
Maseru Lesotho 99 E7
Mashhad Iran 109 H3
Massachusetts (State)
USA 27 F5
Massif Central France
63 E6
Matadi Zaire 95 D7
Maturín Venezuela 44 E3
Maun Botswana 99 D5
Mauritania (Country)
92 C4
Mauritius (Country)
101 D6
Mayotte (I.) France 101 C5
Mazār-e Sharif
Aghanistan 111 E5
Mazyr Belorussia 81 F7
Mbabane Swaziland 99 F6
Mbandaka Zaire 95 E6
Mbeya Tanzania 97 E5
Mbuji-Mayi Zaire 95 F7
Mead, Lake USA 34 D4
Mecca Saudi Arabia
108 D5
Medan Indonesia 126 A5
Medellín Colombia 44 B3
Mediterranean Sea 52 G4/
61 F7/63/73/88/90 C2/
104 /106 C4
Meerut India 117 E3
Mekong (R.) Asia 100 G3/
119 E7/121 B5/124 D4/
125 F6
Melaka Malaysia 125 E8
Melbourne Australia
133 F7

Melville I. Canada 23 E3/
51 F4
Memphis USA 28 D3
Mendoza Argentina 49 B5
Mérida Mexico 39 H6
Mérida Venezuela 44 C3
Mersin Turkey 105 E6
Mesa USA 34 D5
Messina Sicily 73 F7
Messina, Strait of Italy
73 G7
Mestre Italy 72 D3
Meta (R.) Colombia/
Venezuela 44 C4
Meuse (R.) Western
Europe 65 D6
Mexicali Mexico 38 D1
Mexico (Country) 38 – 39
Mexico, Gulf of USA 29 E6
Mexico City Mexico 39 F6
Michigan (State) USA
31 F3
Michigan, Lake USA
31 F4
Micronesia, Federated
States of (Country)
128 D4
Middleburg Netherlands
64 C4
Midway Is. USA 129 E3
Milan Italy 72 C3
Milos (I.) Greece 79 F6
Milwaukee USA 31 F5
Minbu Burma 124 B4
Mindano (I.) Philippines
127 F4
Mindoro (I.) Philippines
127 E2
Minho (R.) Portugal 60 C2
Minneapolis USA 30 D4
Minnesota (State) 30 D2
Minorca Balearic Is. Spain
61 H4
Minsk Belorussia 81 E6

R

Rabat Morocco 88 D2
Rach Gia Vietnam 125 F6
Rajkot India 116 D4
Rajshahi Bangladesh
117 G4
Raleigh USA 29 G3
Ranchi India 117 F4
Rangoon Burma
100 F4/125 C5
Rasht Iran 109 F2
Rat Buri Thailand 125 D5
Rawalpindi Pakistan
117 E1
Reşiţa Romania 76 B4
Recife Brazil 47 H5
Red (R.) China/Vietnam
124 E3
Red Sea 90 E4/100 C3/
108 D5
Redding USA 37 B5
Regina Canada 23 F8
Reno USA 34 C2
Resistencia Argentina
48 E4
Reykavik Iceland 52 E3
Rheims France 63 F2
Rhine (R.) W. Europe
64 F4/66 C7/68 C4
Rhode I. (State) USA
27 G5
Rhodes (I.) Greece 79 H7
Rhône (R.) W. Europe
63 F6/68 B6
Richmond USA 29 G2
Riga Latvia 80 D4
Riga, Gulf of Estonia/
Latvia 80 D4
Rîmnicu Vîlcea Romania
76 D4
Río Cuarto Argentina
49 C5
Rio de Janeiro Brazil
47 G6/52 D6

Río Grande (R.) Mexico
39 F3
Rio Grande USA 35 F6
Riverside USA 37 D8
Rivne Ukraine 84 C3
Riyadh Saudi Arabia
109 E5
Roanoke USA 29 G2
Rochester USA 27 E4
Rockford USA 31 E5
Rocky Mts. N. America
22 D6/35 E4
Romania (Country) 76
Rome Italy 73 D5
Rosario Argentina
49 D5
Rostock (Germany) 66 F3
Rostov-na-Donu Rus.
Fed. 83 B6/112 B5
Rotterdam Netherlands
52 F4/64 D4
Rouen France 63 E2
Rovuma (R.) C. Africa
98 H4
Rub' al Khali Saudi
Arabia 109 E7
Ruse Bulgaria 77 E5
Russian Federation
(Country) 81 B5/
82 – 83/ 112 – 113
Rwanda (Country) 96 D4
Ryazan' Rus. Fed. 83 C5/
112 C4

S

Saarbrücken Germany
67 C6
Sabah Malaysia 126 D5
Sabhā Libya 89 G4
Sacramento USA 37 B6
Sagaing Burma 124 C3
Sahara (Desert) N. Africa
88 – 89/92 – 93
Sahel West Africa 93 E5

Sakhalin (I.) Rus. Fed.
112 H5
Salem USA 36 B4
Salt Lake City USA
34 D2
Salta Paraguay 48 C3
Salton Sea USA 37 E8
Salvador Brazil 47 H5
Salween (R.) Burma/
China 119 E7/121 B5/
124 C4
Salzburg Austria 69 F3
Samar (I.) Philippines
127 F3
Samara Rus. Fed.
83 D6/112 C5
Samarinda Indonesia
126 D6
Samarkand Uzbekistan
111 E4
Sambre (R.) Belgium/
France 65 D6
Samos (I.) Greece 79 G5
Samsun Turkey 105 F3
San'a Yemen 109 E8
San Antonio USA 35 G7
San Bernardo Chile 49 B5
San Diego USA 37 D8
San Francisco USA 37 B6
San José Costa Rica 42 C7
San Jose USA 37 B7
San Juan Puerto Rico
43 G5
San Luis Potosí Mexico
39 F5
San Marino (Country)
72 D4
San Miguel de Tucumán
Argentina 48 C4
San Salvador de Jujuy
Paraguay 48 C3
San Salvador El Salvador
42 B5
Sanandaj Iran 109 F2

Acknowledgements

Dorling Kindersley would like to thank:
Hilary Bird, Helen Chamberlain, Tricia Grogan, and Michael Williams for the index; Kate Eager and Tony Chung for design assistance; Sasha Heseltine for editorial assistance; Caroline Brooke and Paul Donnellon for editorial research; James Mills-Hicks and Yak El-Droubie for cartographic assistance;

Picture credits: t=top b=bottom c=centre l=left r=right
The publisher would like to thank the following for their kind permission to reproduce the photographs:

NASA, 13 tr; Science Photo Library/David Parker 15 br.

Every effort has been made to trace the copyright holders and we apologise in advance for any unintentional omissions. We would be pleased to insert the appropriate acknowledgement in any subsequent edition of this publication.